THE
NEW YORKER
75th Anniversary
CARTOON
COLLECTION

THE
NEW YORKER
75th Anniversary
CARTOON COLLECTION

EDITED BY
BOB MANKOFF

POCKET BOOKS

New York   London   Toronto   Sydney   Tokyo   Singapore

POCKET BOOKS, a division of Simon & Schuster Inc.
1230 Avenue of the Americas, New York, NY 10020

ISBN: 0-671-03555-X

First Pocket Books hardcover printing November 1999

10 9 8 7 6 5 4 3 2 1

POCKET and colophon are registered trademarks of Simon & Schuster Inc.

Book design by Laura Lindgren and Celia Fuller

Printed in the U. S. A.

To the constant commitment of
THE NEW YORKER
to this ridiculous and sublime art form.

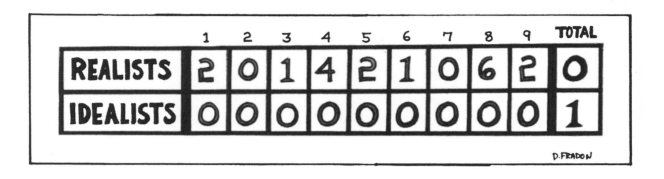

	1	2	3	4	5	6	7	8	9	TOTAL
REALISTS	2	0	1	4	2	1	0	6	2	0
IDEALISTS	0	0	0	0	0	0	0	0	0	1

D. FRADON

To make a book easy to look at, you have to work hard. No one worked harder than Jane Cavolina at Pocket Books. From the get-go, she was able to go get whatever I needed to move the project along. She most often got it from her colleagues at Pocket Books: Emily Bestler, Donna O'Neill, Lisa Feuer, Linda Dingler, Erin Galligan, and Twisne Fan (yes, that's her real name).

Over at *The New Yorker*, I counted on Anne Hall, who has been indispensable to the art of cartooning for twenty-five years, and Emily Votruba, who has been indispensable for two, to add some method to my madness. The collaboration worked perfectly, with me becoming more methodical while they became progressively more mad.

I am also deeply indebted (the check is in the mail) to *The New Yorker* imaging department, headed by perfectionist Greg Captain, for transforming all those old images using all this new technology. For them, good enough wasn't good enough, and that's good enough for me.

Finally, I want to thank my friend Jack Ziegler for all the amazing, arduous, painstaking work he did on this book that I should have done.

INTRODUCTION

NOW ME, you couldn't pay me to read an introduction to a cartoon book. I'd jump straight to the cartoons. You could, however, pay me to write one. Even so, I'm still tempted to stop writing and jump ahead. More than tempted, actually. I'll be back in a minute; wait right here...

Okay. I'm back now, ready to blurb my brains out.

Incidentally, pretesting of this book has shown that 24 percent of you joined me in that first excursion and never returned to this introduction. Frankly, I wish I could do likewise, especially if you're looking at Peter Arno's most popular cartoon, on page 43 (66.2 percent of you are now gone for good), Charles Barsotti's funniest, on page 50 (72.85 percent), or anything by George Booth (it's up to 85.96 percent now). I'm not even going to mention Roz Chast. By not even mentioning her, I know I lost another 14 percent.

For the .0313 percent of you who are still left, some background:

As cartoon editor of *The New Yorker* I help select great cartoons from great cartoonists for a great publication, which has produced the greatest magazine cartooning of the century. Isn't that just great? In addition to being cartoon editor, I'm also a cartoonist myself. I go by the pen name of Mankoff, which unfortunately for me is the same as my real name. Rumor has it that media watchdogs are on the verge of putting two and two together and charging me with conflict of interest.

In a move sure to trigger new investigations, I got to choose cartoons from the entire seventy-five-year history of *The New Yorker*, to create a collection of the crème de la crème of the crème de la crème.

As divine payback for this outrageous good fortune, I'm sure there's a bullet with my name on it somewhere, or maybe just a tainted container of crème de la crème.

There are seven hundred and seven cartoons in this book, the most in any *New Yorker* collection ever. And, all along, the idea was to make this collection the best. But how could I be sure of that when the inclusion of seven hundred and seven cartoons meant the exclusion of more than sixty thousand others?

Well, to start with, I reviewed all *The New Yorker*'s cartoons—close to sixty-one thousand of them. How? With the help of powerful computers that were not only Y2K compliant but obsequious as well.

I then tentatively divided the cartoons into groups: "Tentatively Yes," "Tentatively No," and "Tentatively Maybe." At this point, I realized I was being too tentative and needed some help and guidance in the selection process. And I got it. First, from my fellow-cartoonists. I asked them what they thought were their best cartoons. They weren't shy about telling me, and they weren't shy about threatening me. Many of their recommendations have been included.

Then I asked a number of *The New Yorker*'s senior editors to search their memories for their favorites. Then I asked them to do it again when they came up with the wrong favorites.

Finally, I asked for suggestions from a source that has never before been used in compiling a *New Yorker* cartoon album: you the reader—or you the surfer, the thirty thousand of you who have registered at *The New Yorker*'s cartoon site (www.cartoonbank.com). Literally hundreds of your choices have been included in this book, and, frankly, if you don't like them you have no one to blame but yourselves.

There's nothing else to say. Which is just as well, because at this point there's probably no one left to say it to. For anybody who still happens to be reading this, enjoy the cartoons and I'll see you later in the Artists' Index under Mankoff.

MANKOFF

New York, 1999

THE
NEW YORKER
75th Anniversary
CARTOON
COLLECTION

"Because it's here, that's why."

"I just dialed 1–800-BAGUETTE."

"Now, this over here, this is why you're going to have to go to jail."

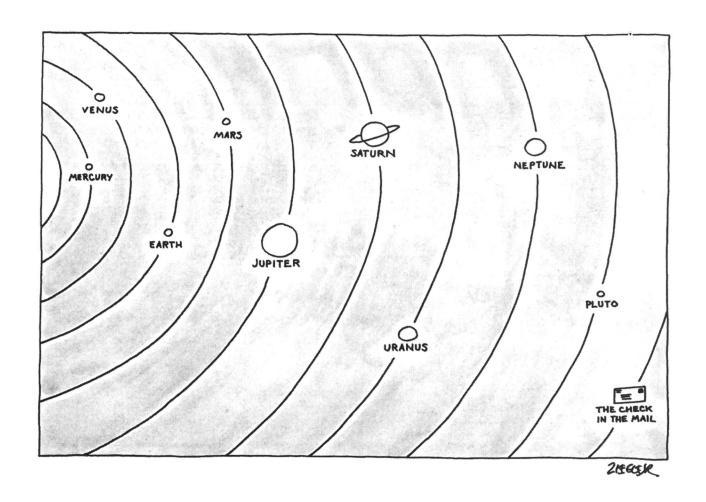

THE CHECK
IN THE MAIL

"Tremaine, could I see you for a moment—alone?"

3

"Please hurry, Hilary. Your soup's getting dirty."

"Artificial coloring, artificial flavoring, artificial glop, artificial slop, artificial this, artificial that . . ."

"Curiosity."

"I sent your dry cleaning to France."

"Why, Hennings, I had no idea."

"It's not enough that we succeed. Cats must also fail."

"Dear no, Miss Mayberry—just the head."

"Now can you hear me—you boys in the back?"

"Your car will be right down, Mr. Lundquist."

"Howard, I think the dog wants to go out."

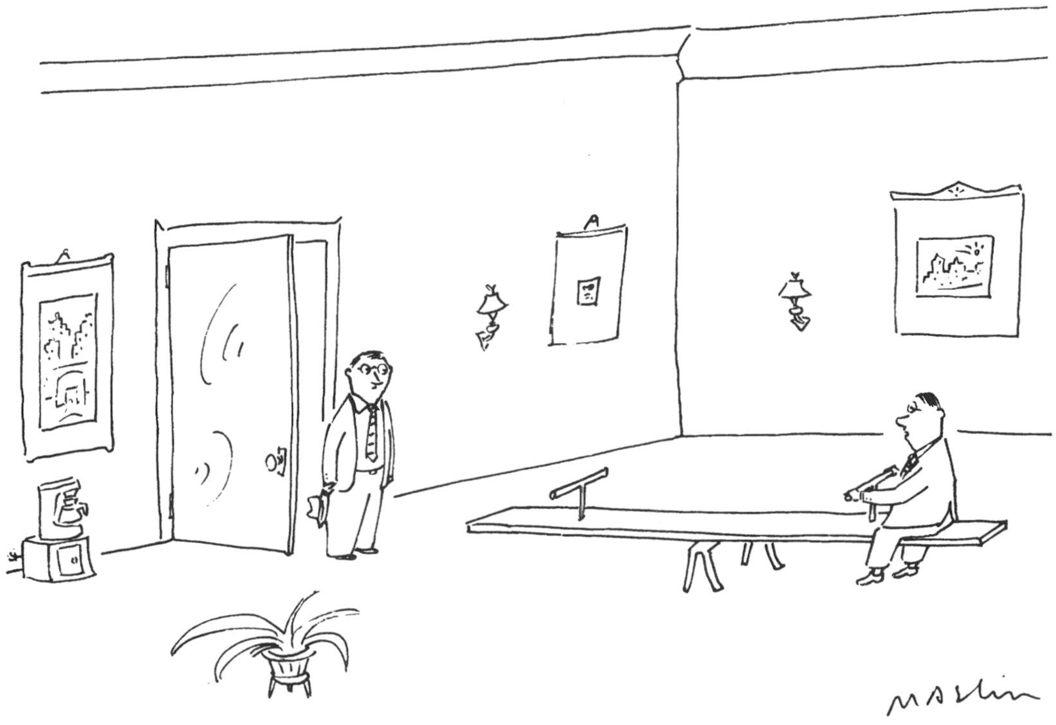

"We'll begin, Mr. Bergeron, just as soon as you're seated."

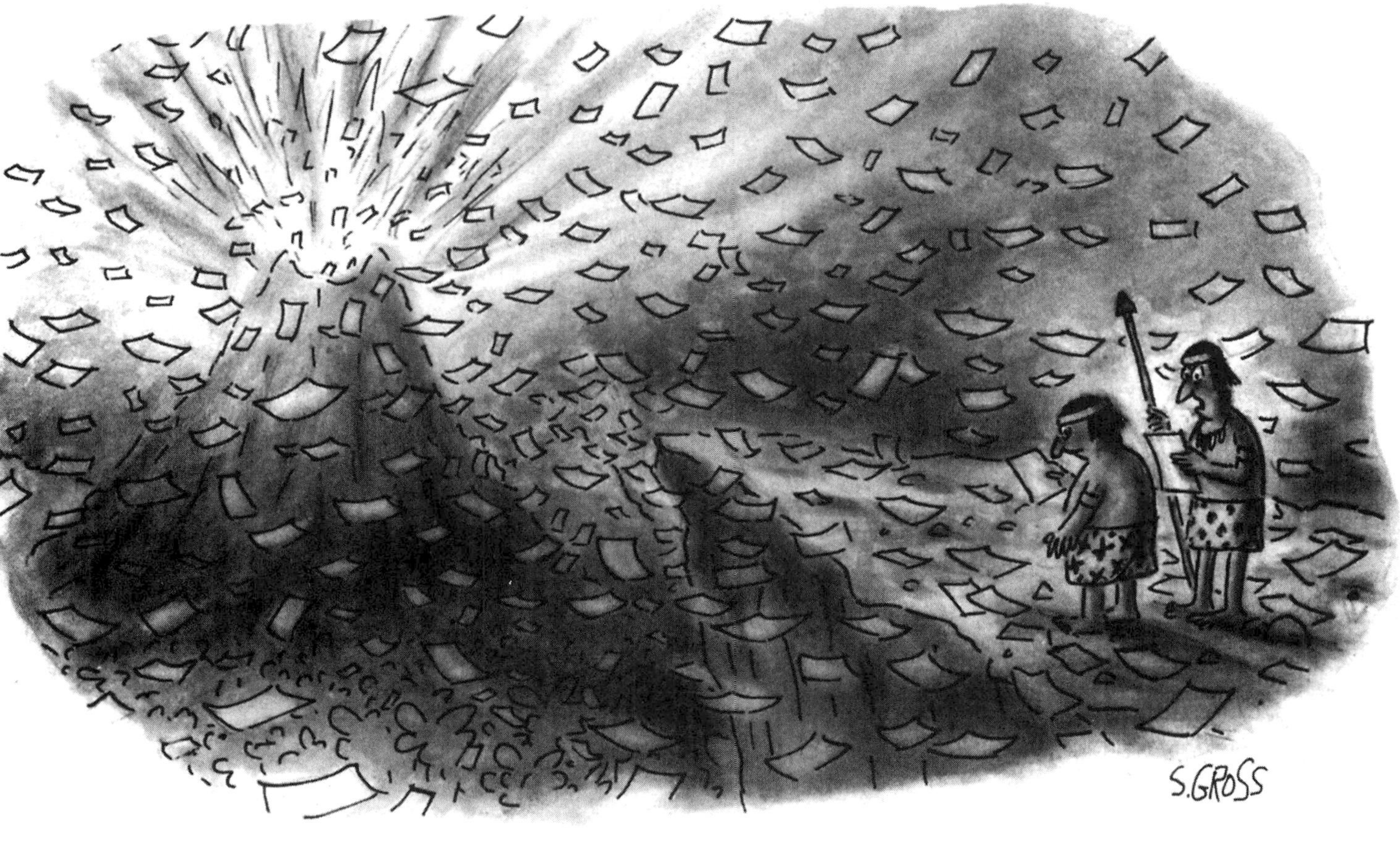

"The gods are distributing Chinese menus."

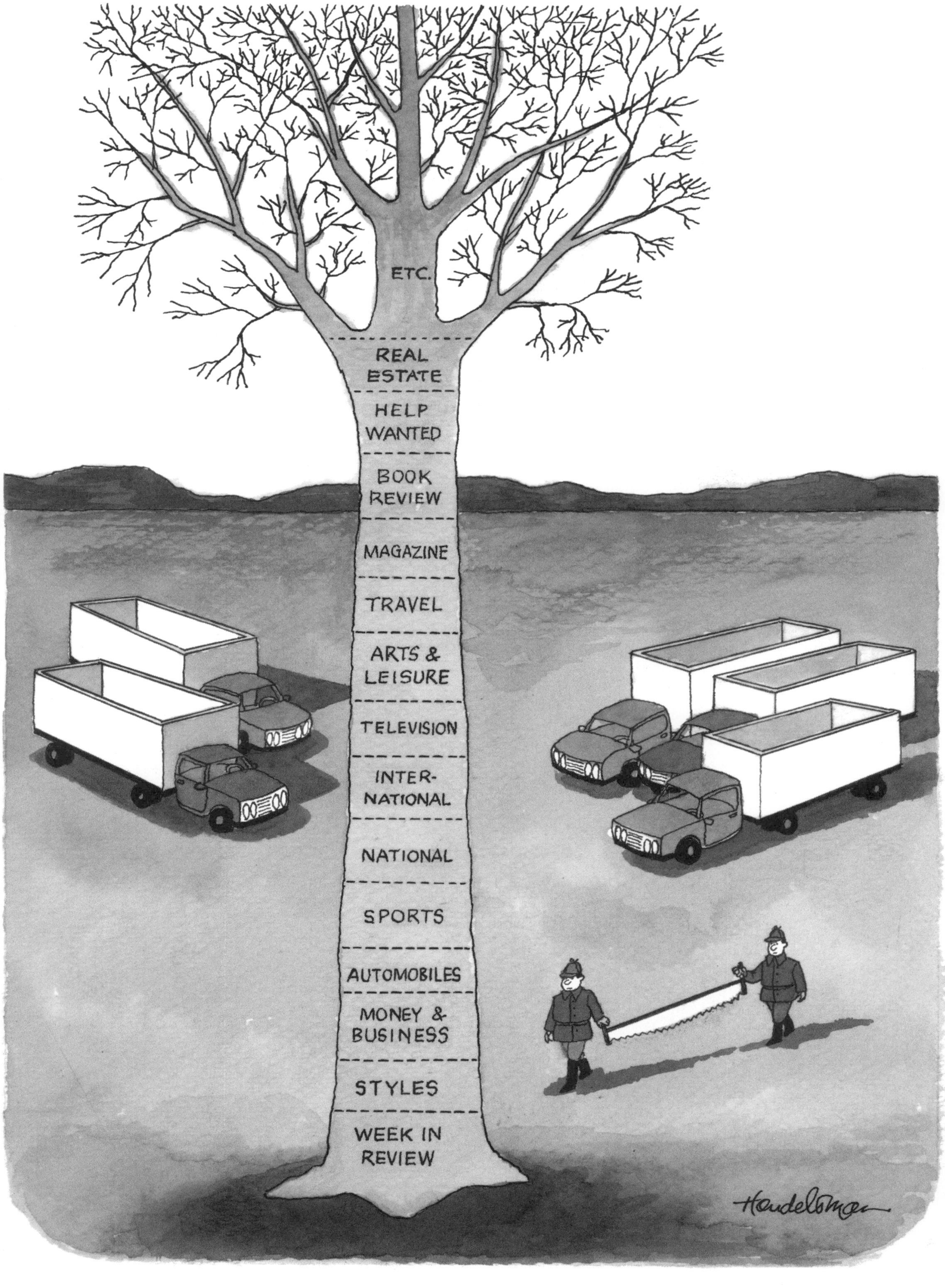
ETC.
REAL ESTATE
HELP WANTED
BOOK REVIEW
MAGAZINE
TRAVEL
ARTS & LEISURE
TELEVISION
INTER-NATIONAL
NATIONAL
SPORTS
AUTOMOBILES
MONEY & BUSINESS
STYLES
WEEK IN REVIEW
Handelsman

"We have to be missing twenty-four hours before I consider us lost."

"My support group told me to go to hell."

Go–Between

"Hey, pal, do you have any idea who I think I am?"

"She's not all over you, but she gets the job done."

"Thou hast eyes to see, and see not!"

"What the hell was I supposed to do? I've been declawed!"

THE CORNER OF OGDEN AND NASH

THE JOURNEY TO ENLIGHT-ENMENT

"Are we there yet?"

"It just seems to me, Howard, that you're missing the whole point of having a terrace in the city."

"'Hold,' young lady, is for other people."

"Death ray, fiddlesticks! Why, it doesn't even slow them up."

*"Sorry—He's changed His mind again. Stripes on the zebra,
spots on the giraffe, no stars on the lion, and make
the elephant bigger and the amoeba smaller."*

*"It's a naïve domestic Burgundy without any breeding,
but I think you'll be amused by its presumption."*

*"Front desk? There are
no little candies on my pillow."*

17

JIMMY, SIXTH-GENERATION PAIN IN THE ASS

"*The town has no history, Signore. It was built from scratch three years ago, entirely for the tourist trade.*"

"He didn't really die of anything.
He was a hypochondriac."

"Not only do you look marvellous
but all of you looks the same age."

THE DOG FORMERLY
KNOWN AS PRINCE

"Back to Square One!"

"They moved my bowl."

"Research and development."

"Same old ice, same old aurora borealis, same old everything!"

"Yeah? Well, I've forgotten more about paleontology than you'll ever know."

"Shouldn't he be lying at the <u>foot</u> of the bed?"

"Could you direct us to Off Broadway?"

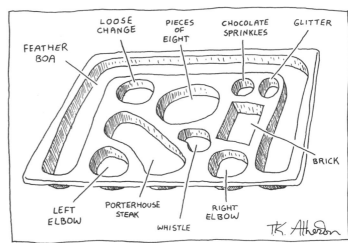

DESK-TOP ORGANIZER

"You'd think George and Ella would try to patch things up for the children's sake."

"You're not at all like your answering machine."

23

"We're here to escape religious persecution. What are you here for?"

"I couldn't disagree with you more. I think yours is greener."

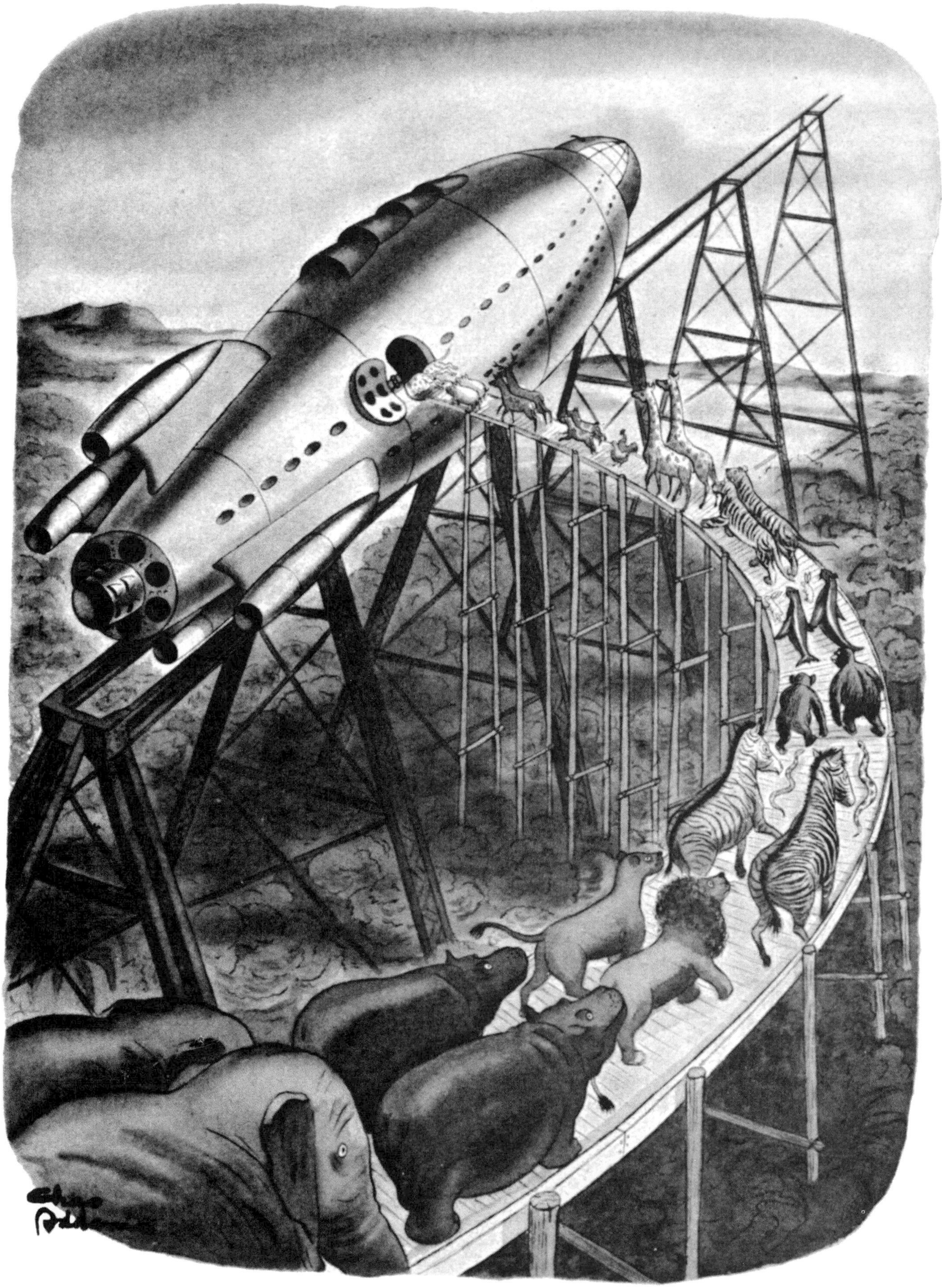

"O.K., the third of July is out. How about the fourth?"

"Why does she want to go back to Kansas,
where everything is in black-and-white?"

IT'S JUST GOING TO CONTINUE AND CONTINUE

"We've found the problem. You folks don't own a car."

"Mr. Speaker, will the gentleman from Small Firearms yield the floor to the gentleman from the Big Tobacco?"

"Well, it makes a difference to me!"

"I couldn't resist—the second pair was free."

"Bob up and down."

"Happy fortieth. I'll take the muscle tone in your upper arms,
the girlish timbre of your voice, your amazing tolerance for caffeine,
and your ability to digest French fries. The rest of you can stay."

"As soon as one problem is solved, another rears its ugly head."

29

"For a while after he retired he was lost.
He didn't know what to do with himself."

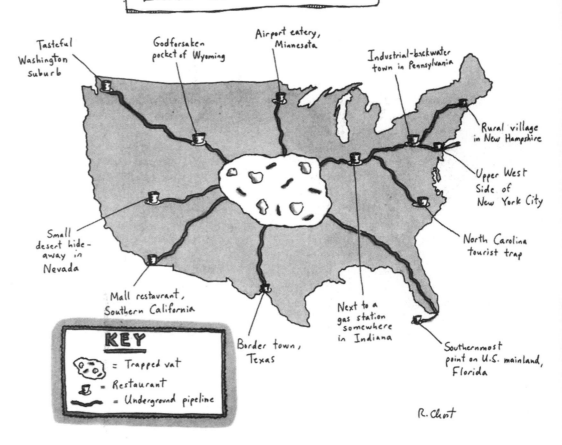

THE HUGE-UNDERGROUND-TRAPPED-VAT
THEORY OF WHY ALL WONTON SOUP TASTES
EXACTLY THE SAME

Tasteful
Washington
suburb

Godforsaken
pocket of Wyoming

Airport eatery,
Minnesota

Industrial-backwater
town in Pennsylvania

Rural village
in New Hampshire

Upper West
Side of
New York City

North Carolina
tourist trap

Small
desert hide-
away in
Nevada

Mall restaurant,
Southern California

Border town,
Texas

Next to a
gas station
somewhere
in Indiana

Southernmost
point on U.S. mainland,
Florida

KEY

= Trapped vat

= Restaurant

= Underground pipeline

R. Chast

"By the way, I'm taking off the first two weeks in August."

"Who's the grownup tonight?"

"Travel is the sherbet between courses of reality."

"I'm sorry, but the flight of the bumblebees has been cancelled."

"It's broccoli, dear."
"I say it's spinach, and I say the hell with it."

"Is there any chance of getting my testicles back?"

Separated at birth, the Mallifert twins meet accidentally.

Shanahan

"My name is Andrew, and I need a ride."

"It's my only vice."

DONNELLY

"Some kids at school called you a feminist,
Mom, but I punched them out."

"What was the name of that tranquillizer we took?"

"I'm afraid we'll have to call it quits, Irene.
I love a parade."

"I dreamed that butter and sugar and eggs
came back, and we all made cookies."

"May I remind the witness that he is under water."

"Scotch and toilet water?"

The Tip of the Iceberg

"It could be worse. He could be out chasing you know what."

"Hickory smoke—that's what gives it
that hearty Western flavor."

"Thank you, Adrian. Parenting is a learning process,
and your criticisms help."

"With you I have known peace, Lida,
and now you say you're going crazy."

"It feels like it might be a grain of sand."

"This toy is designed to hasten the child's adjustment to the world around him. No matter how carefully he puts it together, it won't work."

"The work being done on your marriage—are you having it done, or are you doing it yourselves?"

"We must be doing seventy easy!"

41

"We had to let the animals go. No one informed them of their rights when they were arrested."

"Did I kiss you hello yet?"

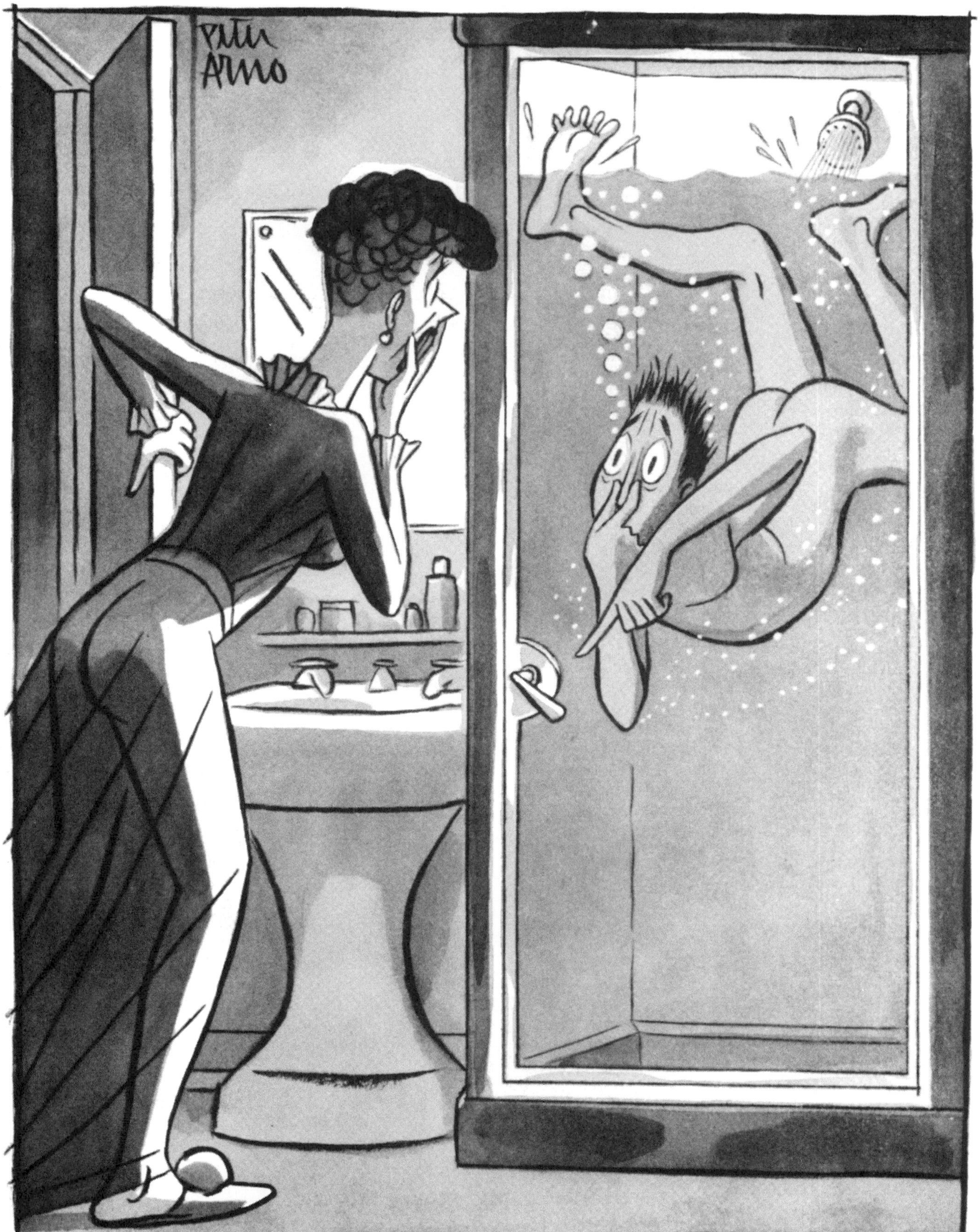
Peter Arno

THEORIES OF EVERYTHING

"Oh, not bad. The light comes on, I press the bar, they write me a check. How about you?"

"Scientists confirmed today that everything we know about the structure of the universe is wrongedy-wrong-wrong."

"As I said earlier, Michelle, I won't answer questions about economic or foreign policy. I'm here to talk about my sexual escapades."

"Don't panic. I'm just a sore throat."

45

"Please! There happens to be a lady present."

*"We are neither hunters nor gatherers.
We are accountants."*

"Mind if I smoke?"

"I didn't actually <u>build</u> it, but it was based on my idea."

"Say 'please.'"

"It was good of you to come, Doctor."

"I sold my soul for about a tenth of what
the damn things are going for now."

"Tonight the part normally played by the audience will be
played by actors playing the part of the audience."

"Fusilli, you crazy bastard! How the hell are you?"

"Miss! Oh, Miss! For God's sake, stop!"

"Hey, big guy. Can I buy you a pair of underpants?"

"Night fell over the land like an L.L. Bean navy-blue summerweight
one-hundred-per-cent-goose-down-filled comforter covering up an Eddie Bauer hunter-green
one-hundred-per-cent-combed-cotton, machine-washable king-size fitted sheet."

THE ETHEL MORMON TABERNACLE CHOIR

"'Season's Greetings' looks O.K. to me.
Let's run it by the legal department."

"O.K., so you're forty, you've lived half your life. Look at the bright side.
If you were a horse, you'd already be dead fifteen years."

"Someday man will find a peaceful use for my machines."

JONIK

W. Steig

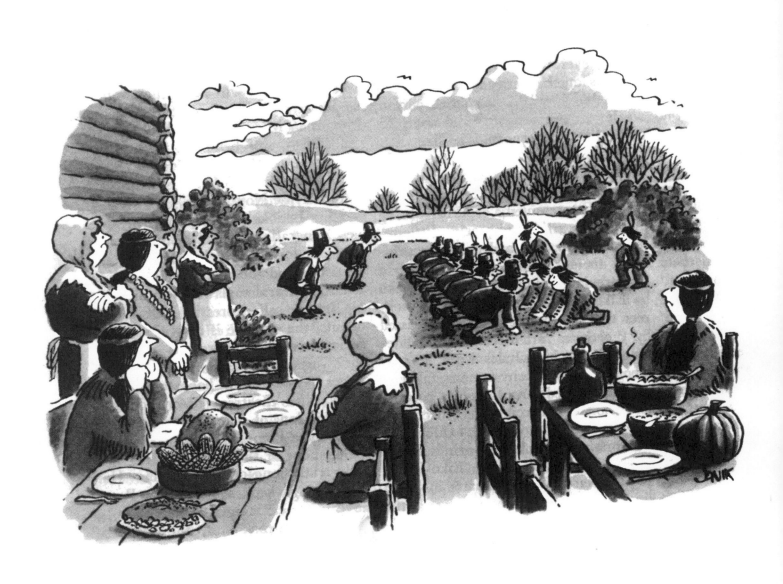

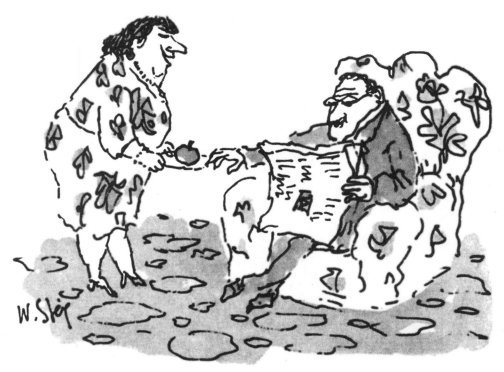

"A little further, dear."

"What I'm proposing is this. No."

"We'll widen the clogged artery by inserting a balloon."

"First, they do an on-line search."

"That's the worst set of opinions
I've heard in my entire life."

"He's, like, 'To be or not to be,' and I'm, like, 'Get a life.'"

"I was a ruthless, driven, unfeeling son of a bitch—and it worked out extremely well."

"I'll throw in a few extra pinstripes."

"I love the idea of there being two sexes, don't you?"

"Of course, what I'd really like to do is direct."

"But how do you know for sure you've got power unless you abuse it?"

1

2

3

*"My dear, perhaps you had better
look over this ending. I don't want to
be guilty of too much levity."*

4

5

6

*"Why, it seems to be all right.
I don't think it's too funny—not at all."*

7

"My question is: Are we making an impact?"

P. BARLOW

S. GROSS

60

"Look! Jim has the ball! See him run! Run, Jim, run!"

"It's like this. If the rich have money, they invest.
If the poor have money, they eat."

"Now, now, Harrison, we all start somewhere."

"I'd invite you in, but my life's a mess."

"I said the National Endowment for the Arts is offering you a hundred and fifty thousand dollars to lie fallow for a year."

"Gee, honey, this place has got everything."

MOM-O-GRAMS

"Hate to bother you, but are you getting our supertitles for 'Rigoletto'?"

"Tonight, we're going to let the statistics speak for themselves."

"Too much purple."

"I _know_ what I said ten minutes ago. That was the _old_ me talking."

65

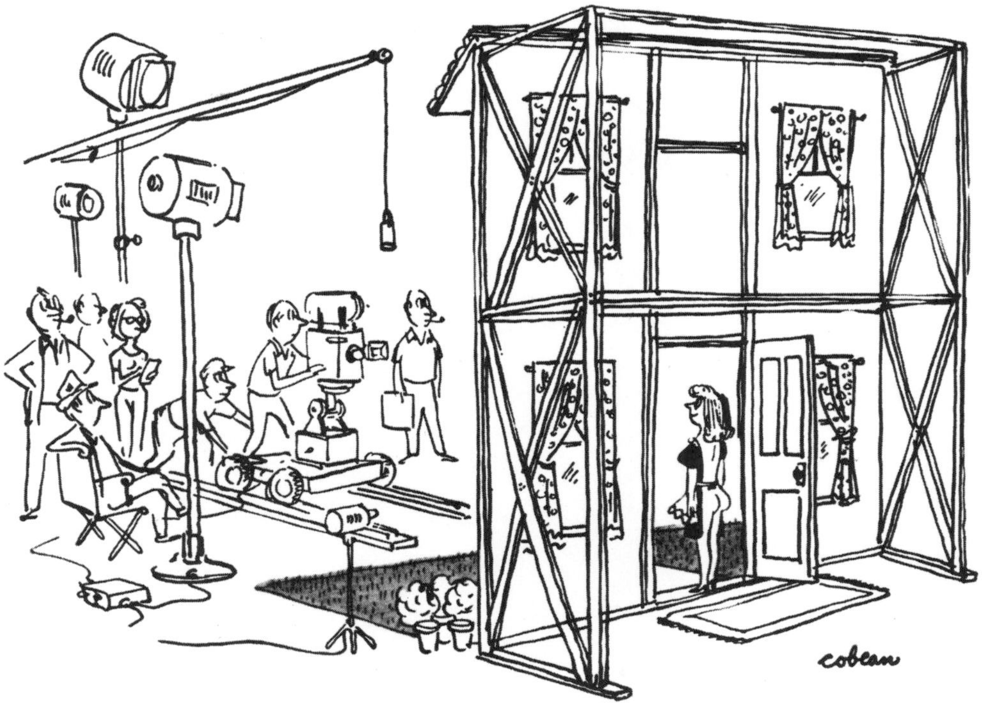
cobean

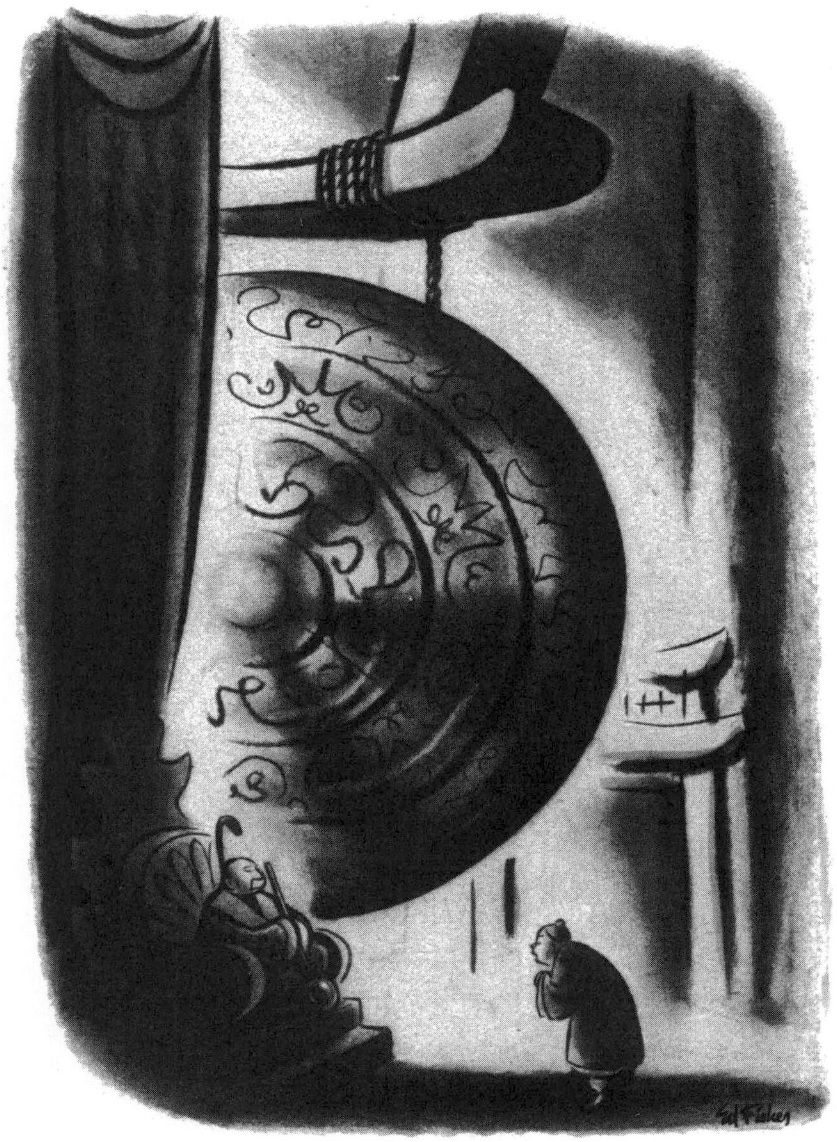

"You rang?"

"Then it's agreed. Judgment Day, whenever it comes, will fall on a Thursday, so that they'll get the long weekend."

"They have your eyes, but their father's hair."

"Now, if you'll just sign right here, Mr. Hark, you'll make the biggest mistake of your life!"

"I certainly hope we don't end up offending Islam."

"Do you ever have one of those days when everything seems unconstitutional?"

*"Has it occurred to you that every time we decide to face basic issues,
all we do is put the house on the market?"*

"We save all the original packaging in case we have to return something."

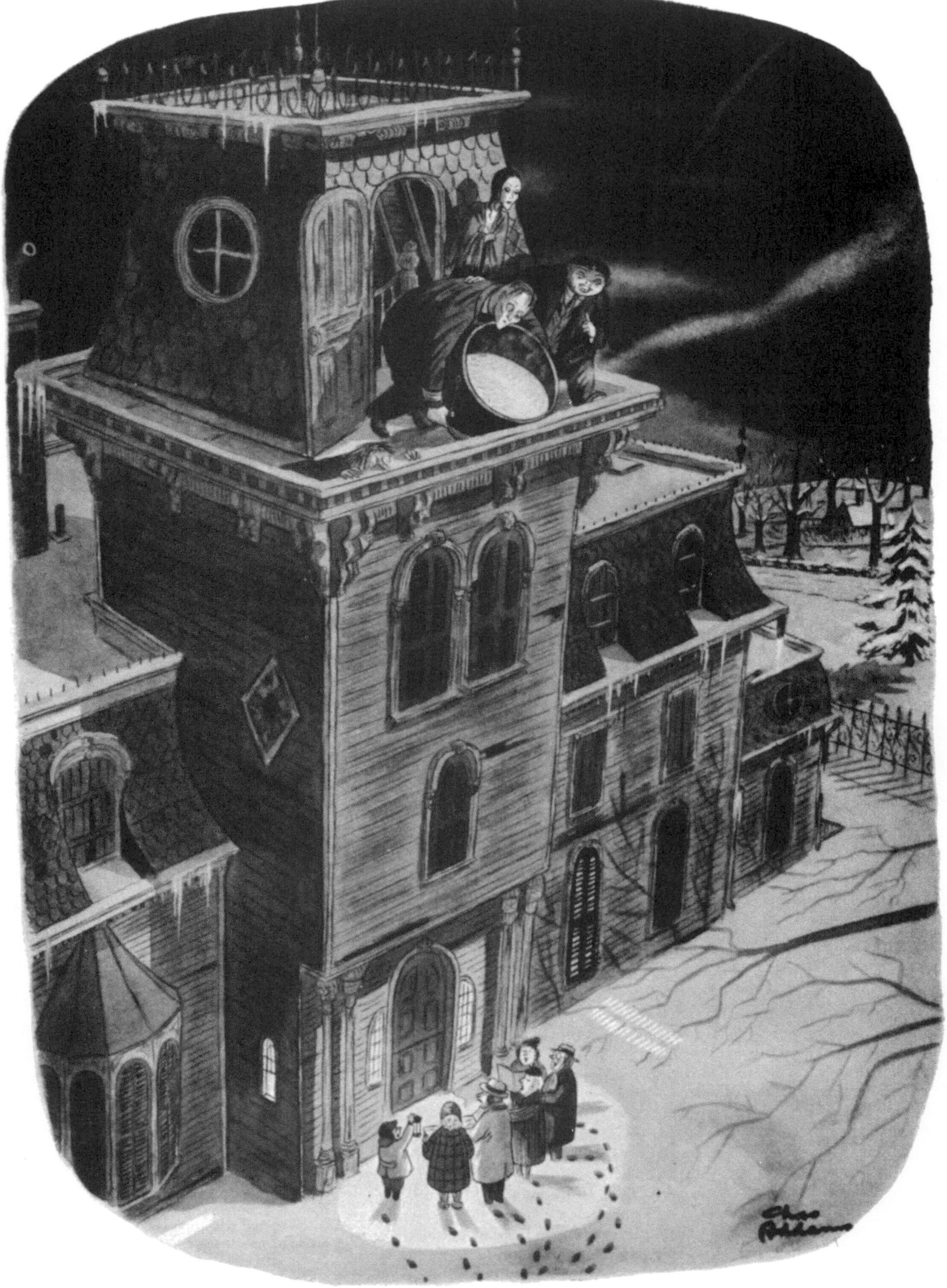
Chas Addams

"Do you think you can manage a smile?
It's only for a fiftieth of a second."

"Oh, Lord! Not _another_ wine-and-cheese party!"

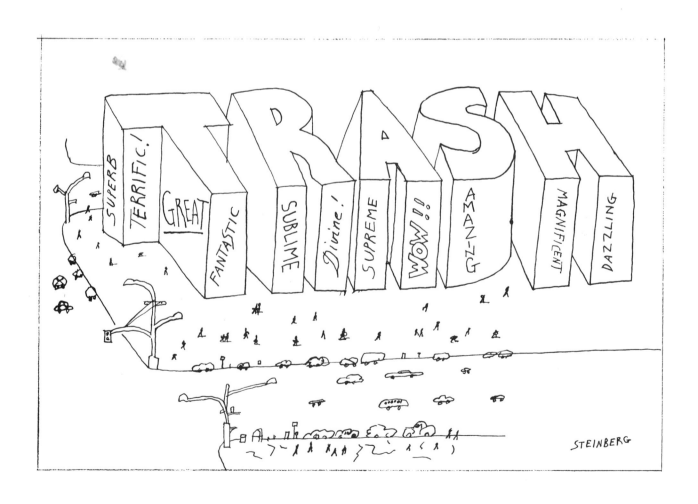

"But does it ever get that cold?"

B. Smaller

"I would share my cookies,
but I'm afraid I'll set up a cycle of dependency."

"Her landlord kicked her cat!
How did this thing ever get out of Small Claims Court?"

"Goodnight moon. Goodnight house. Goodnight breasts."

"My advice is to learn all the tricks
you can while you're young."

INFORMATION-AGE LOSERS

THE I.R.S. CHANNEL

INTERACTIVE WELDING

VIRTUAL VIDEO

"That's it, Henry—you've dialed your last mattress!"

"He's about five feet six, has big brown eyes and curly blond hair, and answers to the name of Master."

"Sorry about this, but I just ran out of sand."

"Look, I'm not blaming you. I'm just suing you."

"Have you any regrets, Captain Hale?
Our readers would like to know."

GIFTS FROM THE
HOUSE OF LOW GOALS

T-Shirts

I SURVIVED CONJUNCTIVITIS

I CAN READ A BUS SCHEDULE

100% HUMAN DNA

Special-Occasion Cakes

WOW! ONLY 6 CAVITIES!

HAPPY TATTOO REMOVAL!

NO LOITERING ARRESTS IN ONE YEAR!

Cards

I'm so glad you're not an arsonist!

CONGRATULATIONS ON YOUR NEW EASY CHAIR!

Trophies

PARTICIPANT

"It was a three-alarm fire—practically gutted the place."

"I swore they'd never take me alive, but when
the time came I figured what the hell."

"Isn't it amazing—everybody has everybody's number
and yet everything keeps going along."

"Ammonia! Ammonia!"

"On the basis of these figures, Carter, your suggestion seems quite sound.

Certainly our expansion program is flexible enough to include these items.

However, on balance I think the proposal is premature.

Now, as to these figures on capital replacement. . . ."

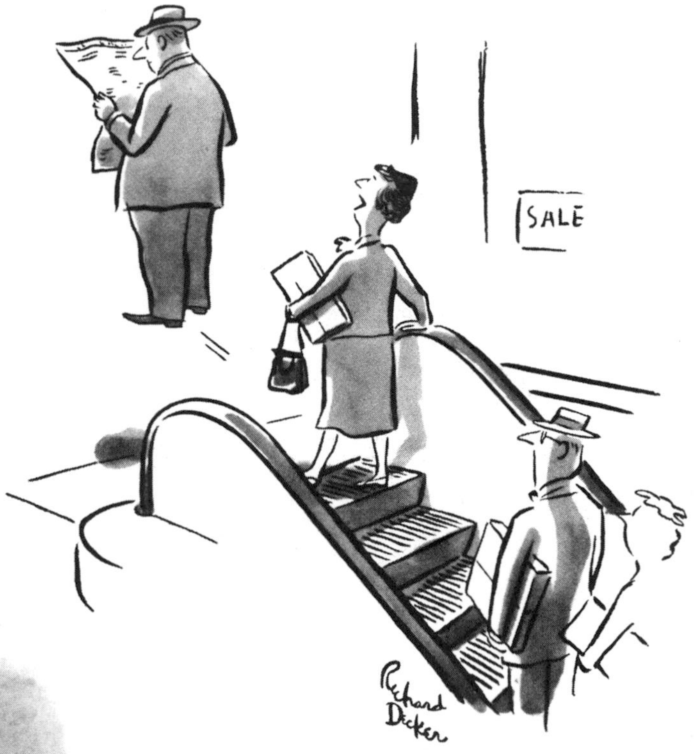
SALE
Richard Decker

"Henry!"

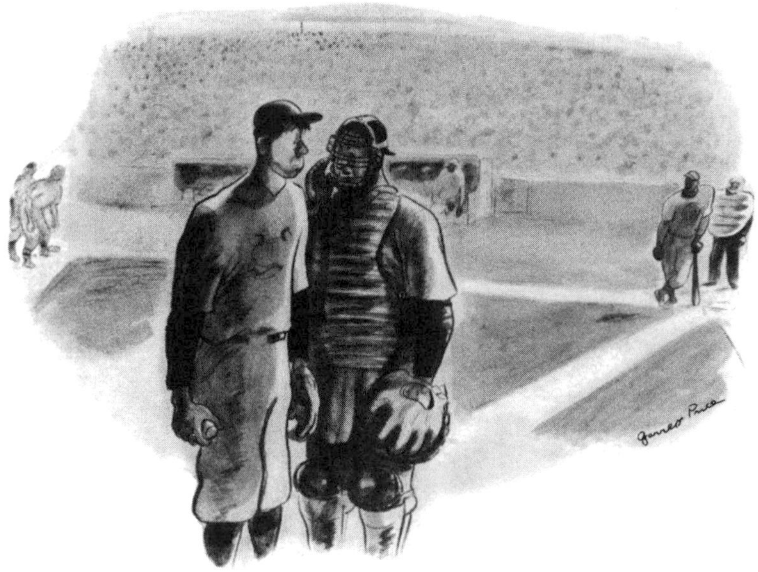

"Strike him out."

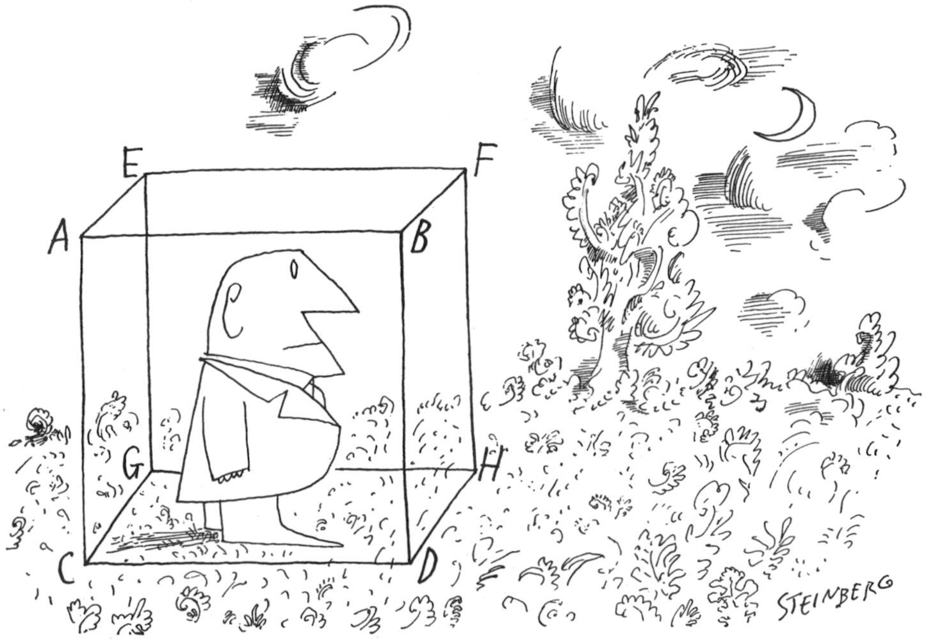
E
F
A
B
G
H
C
D
STEINBERG

"I found the old format much more exciting."

"Why, no, Ken—I don't want to talk about it."

"English lit—how about you?"

"Bon pillage!"

"I think he's just stewed."

"Miss Andrews, take a postcard."

"I'm afraid we'll need more time to fight for the check."

"Harry, take it from me. You're doing yourself more harm than good."

83

"I love coffee, I love tea. I love the girls, an' the girls love me."

*"What do you mean 'Your guess is as good as mine'?
My guess is a hell of a lot <u>better</u> than your guess!"*

DONNA KARAN'S NIGHTMARE

"Whenever Mother's Day rolls around, I regret having eaten my young."

"Do you want that with or without angioplasty?"

"Surely, Son, you can find something to paint indoors."

"When he leaves, I'm in charge."

"Because of illness, the role of Mimi in tonight's performance will be sung by a temp."

"Gee, Jack! That was very careless of you."

S. GROSS

"I don't care if she is a tape dispenser. I love her."

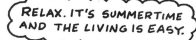

"O.K., I'm sitting. What is it?"

"I told him it wouldn't kill him to try to be nice once in a while, but I was wrong."

BACK HOME AGAIN
IN INDIANA

"I don't mind your acting as your own attorney, but would you please stop hopping on and off that damned chair?"

"There's someone I'd like you to meet."

BEWARE
OF DOG

"George! George! Drop the keys!"

"Well, that's that. When's the next comet?"

"Art, you're beautiful, but you have three minutes."

"Because I've already said all I can say in this particular medium."

"No, no, that's not a sin, either. My goodness, you must have worried yourself to death."

"That's the kind of garbage I have to listen to all the time."

"Paper or plastic?"

"Wait! Come back! I was just kidding about wanting to be happy."

"A grand jury sitting in Terre Haute, Indiana,
today handed up an indictment of society."

"Getting much flak from Women's Lib?"

"It was right where you left it—under the table."

"Waiter! My glass is half empty."

WHY THE BALL IS JUMPING OUT

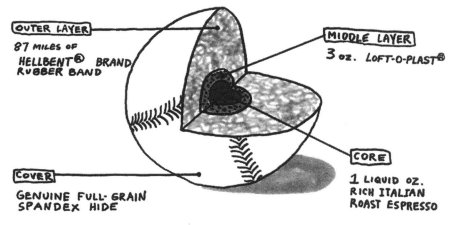

OUTER LAYER
87 MILES OF
HELLBENT® BRAND
RUBBER BAND

MIDDLE LAYER
3 OZ. LOFT-O-PLAST®

COVER
GENUINE FULL-GRAIN
SPANDEX HIDE

CORE
1 LIQUID OZ.
RICH ITALIAN
ROAST ESPRESSO

"I'm taking out two acres of pecan trees and putting in a
fifteen-thousand-square-foot colonic-irrigation facility."

97

EGGS BENEDICT ARNOLD

"Would you please remove your license from your collar?"

DIARY OF A CAT

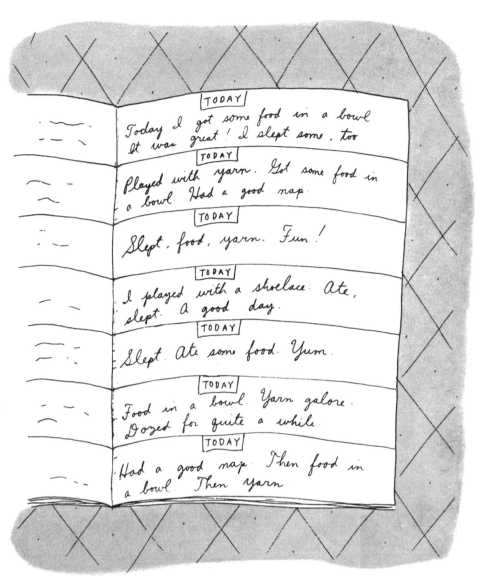

TODAY

Today I got some food in a bowl.
It was great! I slept some, too.

TODAY

Played with yarn. Got some food in
a bowl. Had a good nap.

TODAY

Slept. food, yarn. Fun!

TODAY

I played with a shoelace. Ate,
slept. A good day.

TODAY

Slept. Ate some food. Yum.

TODAY

Food in a bowl. Yarn galore.
Dozed for quite a while.

TODAY

Had a good nap. Then food in
a bowl. Then yarn.

R. Chast

"That banquet was most delicious, and yet now, somehow, once again I feel the pang of hunger."

"We just haven't been flapping them hard enough."

"We're borrowing the best features of the Canadian system."

ELOISE REVISITED

I am Eloise
I am forty-six
I *still* live at The Plaza
I don't give a damn who owns it

"*Now read me the part again where I disinherit everybody.*"

WHAT LEMMINGS BELIEVE

"After all these years, you still feel guilt?
You should be ashamed of yourself."

"Lily is the child. Violet is the dog."

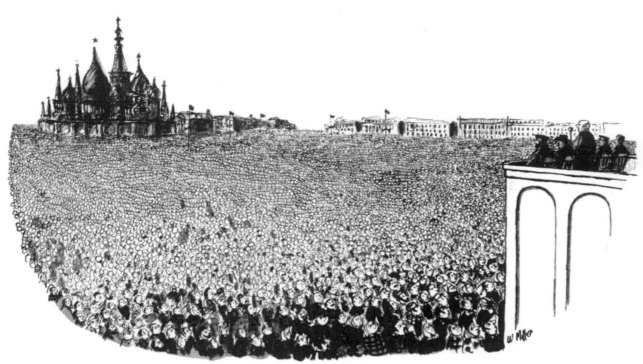

"You're probably wondering why we asked you here today."

"It started out with lactose, but now he's intolerant of _everything_."

"What with the population crunch and all,
we're just reproducing ourselves and letting it go at that."

"That's the Hudson River School, son."

"We located the hissing noise, Mr. Watkins. Your wife's mother is in the back seat."

"I knew you'd like this place."

"Well, Stoddard, I think I've bounced
enough ideas off you for one day."

"You're right—it _doesn't_ have a blade!"

*"It's a damned outrage, Faversham.
Do you realize that in a mere fifteen years
we've gone from fifty-five to seventy?"*

*"Let me take you away from all this
and bring you over to all that."*

"You have an inordinately long shelf life, for a cupcake."

"Money is life's report card."

"Don't worry. They'll be out by the tenth."

"What do you say we call this the end of Date One,
and just start Date Two?"

"I don't sing because I am happy.
I am happy because I sing."

"Supper's almost ready.
I hope you didn't just grab a hot dog for lunch."

"Are you sure you _wore_ a hat?"

"No, I don't know where your pirate shirt is."

"Why, Harriet, I hardly recognized you!"

"Isn't it sort of great when it turns out a couple like that really _was_ too good to be true?"

"Everything's so easy for you, Mr. Perfect."

"Well, back to the old drawing board."

"We're neither software nor hardware. We're your parents."

"I'll quit when it stops being fun."

"I'll thank you, Madam, not to squeeze the tomatoes."

"Who <u>asked</u> you to share my interests?"

"You know what I'd like to try someday? Landlubbing."

*"If Anderson is C.E.O., and Wyatt is C.F.O., and you're C.O.O.,
then who am I, and what am I doing here?"*

*"Since you have already been convicted by the media,
I imagine we can wrap this up pretty quickly."*

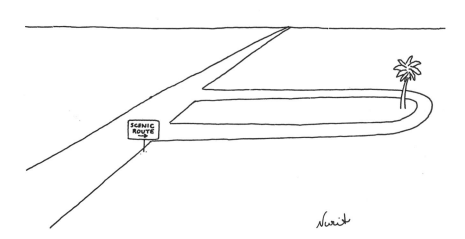

"I realize that those of you who are planning to go into psychiatry may find this dull."

"But can they save themselves?"

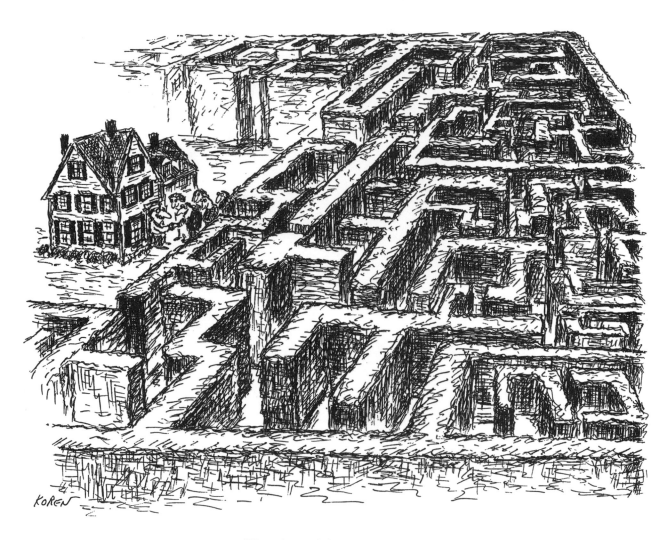

"Your instructions were perfect."

"Oops! Wrong plug."

"Au secours!
Sauvez-moi!
Au secours!"

"If he's not a Frenchman he's certainly an awful snob."

THIS STRUCTURE WILL BE TORN DOWN AND REPLACED BY A NEW 44-STORY COOKIE

THE FOUR AGES OF MAN

INFANCY   CHILDHOOD   YOUTH   MATURITY

THE 60-HOUR GOURMET

RECIPES FOR PEOPLE WHO HAVE TIME TO SPARE, AND THEN SOME

Painstakin' Peas

Before cooking, peel six hundred peas. Boil. Then arrange in a festive manner on a serving platter.

Never-Ending Bread

Mix bread dough as usual. Let rise until double. Punch down. Let rise again. Punch down. Let rise. Punch down. Let rise. Punch down. Rise. Punch. Rise, punch, rise, punch, rise. Bake and serve.

Slow 'n' Steady Chicken

Wash chicken in a lukewarm bubble bath for ± one hour. Then rinse for thirty minutes. Stuff with Difficult Stuffing*, using a doll spoon, and truss with an itsy-bitsy needle and the teensy-weensiest stitch you can. Cook at 125°F. for 32 hours. Just prior to serving, carve into the shape of a rose.

* see page 883

Handmade Carrot Juice

Begin by mincing raw carrots with a butter knife. Then keep going until the whole thing reaches a liquid consistency.

R. Chast

"High inside. Ball three. Count is now three balls and two strikes. Here comes the pitch."

"He thinks he's so great!"

"Dear Aunt Frieda: Thank you very much for the large book. . . ."

"Is this a good time to bring up a car problem?"

"Discouraging data on the antidepressant."

"Don't you understand? This is _life_, this is what is happening.
We _can't_ switch to another channel."

"How will you ever know whether you're a
flying squirrel if you don't give it a shot?"

"We're encouraging people to become involved in their own rescue."

EMERGENCY
INSTRUCTIONS

1. Grab your coat
and get your hat.
2. Leave your worry
on the doorstep.
3. Just direct your
feet to the sunny
side of the street.

"Some women to see you, Anne."

"No, no, no! _Thirty_ days hath September!"

LIFE WITHOUT MOZART

"Can't you see I'm trying to train an elephant?"

"Would everyone check to see they have an attorney? I seem to have ended up with two."

126

FROM THE TOURNAMENT OF NEUROSES PARADE

The "I Never Really Broke Away from My Parents" Float

The "In My Mind's Eye, I Will Always Be a Fat, Short, Frizzy-Haired, Glasses-and-Braces-Wearing Sixth Grader" Float

The "People Who Have Difficulty Forming Bonds of Intimacy with Other People" Float

The "I Only Want What Is Unattainable" Float

The "Hypochondria" Float

The "Fear of Chickens" Float

R. Chast

"Be frank, Jan. Do I look ousted?"

"I don't love you anymore, Lucille,
and I'm dropping you off at your mother's house."

THE FOUR MAJOR FOOD GROUPS

Regular:

Hamburger, cola, French fries, fruit pie.

Company:

Cracker variety, canapé, "interesting" cheese, mint.

Remorse:

Plain yogurt, soybeans, mineral water, tofu

Silly:

Space-food sticks, gelatine mold with fruit salad in it, grasshopper pie.

R. Chast

"You might want to sit down, Mrs. Dumpty."

J B Modell

"*I'm telling you the truth, sweetie—the stork brought you.*"

PLEASE DO NOT KNOCK OR RING DOORBELL

"Frankly, I think we'll regret introducing these organisms into the environment."

"It's pretty simple, Jimmy. We get you some ice cream and then we throw you off the Verrazano. You got a problem with that?"

131

"Its DNA is consistent with meat loaf."

"We have as much fun as ever, but we've learned
how to cram it all in by eleven."

"Your father and I want to explain why we've decided to live apart."

"Achilles! How's the wife? The kids? The heel?"

"Sometimes it's important to stop whatever break you're taking and just do the work."

LASSIE! GET HELP!!

"Note the small zipper pocket of your sales kit. It contains a cyanide capsule."

"I thought I heard a twig snap."

"I've done it again."

"You can't legislate morality, thank heaven."

"Perhaps _this_ will refresh your memory."

"You don't get an office. You get cargo pants."

"Mrs. Hammond! I'd know you anywhere from little Billy's portrait of you."

DISCOVERING THAT THE LIGHT AT THE
END OF THE TUNNEL IS NEW JERSEY

"You may switch to the less expensive wine now."

THE DECAFÉ

"When was the last time you started her up?"

"There's a twenty in it for you if you just keep moving."

"And, of course, when the King said
'A horse, a horse! my kingdom for a horse!'
you assumed he was serious?"

"There you are!"

"Be patient, Madam. The judging of the funny hats will resume as soon as we get ashore."

"My baby is not on backwards—
your baby is on backwards."

DESCENT INTO THE MAELSTROM

SIX HOURS IN THE CAR WITH...

DAD • **MOM** • **TIMMY** • **JUDY**

HOUR ONE

JUDY: I'm hungry.

MOM: How can you be hungry? We just left the house.

TIMMY: I'm cold.

DAD: You're not cold. It's 90° outside.

JUDY: Are we there yet?

HOUR TWO

DAD: Whoever sees an animal first gets 50¢.

JUDY: Look! There's a bug on the windshield! I get 50¢!

TIMMY: That's not an *animal*, that's an *insect*, you dork.

JUDY: Insects *ARE* animals, jerk.

TIMMY: But that doesn't mean they *COUNT*.

JUDY: Dad? Do insects count?

MOM: Why don't we all enjoy this beautiful scenery?

HOUR THREE

TIMMY: Leave me alone.

JUDY: What am I *DOING???*

TIMMY: Your foot just touched my foot.

MOM: You guys are not allowed to *look* at each other, *speak* to each other, or *touch* each other. *IS THAT CLEAR???*

TIMMY: (something under breath).

JUDY: **MOM!!!!!**

HOUR FOUR

DAD: *IF THERE IS ANY MORE NONSENSE FROM BACK THERE, I WILL PULL OVER AND SPANK YOU BOTH TILL YOU SEE STARS! SO HELP ME GOD!!* **THE END!!!!!**

MOM: Look at that old barn over there.

HOUR FIVE

TIMMY: Guess what? We haven't had our seat belts on this whole time!

MOM AND DAD: *PUT YOUR SEAT BELTS ON RIGHT THIS MINUTE!*

HOUR SIX

TIMMY: Let's play Smashies.

JUDY: What's Smashies?

TIMMY: It's when you put your hand on top of the cooler and I try to smash it.

JUDY: Like this?

TIMMY: (SMASH).

JUDY: *OW!* That hurt!

TIMMY: Wanna play Pinchies?

MOM: Does anybody want some grapes?

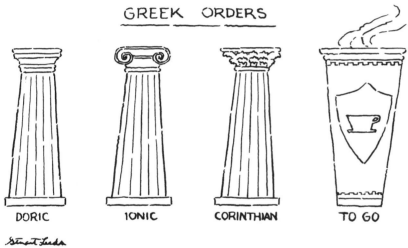

GREEK ORDERS

DORIC   IONIC   CORINTHIAN   TO GO

"I just got damn well fed up with being formal all the time."

145

"Oh, I think I can be principled when necessary."

"You've been very bad,
so we're sending you back to New York."

"The jury will disregard the witness's last remarks."

"Harry wasn't born great and he hasn't achieved greatness,
but he figures there is always the chance that greatness may be thrust upon him."

"You abducted him—*you* feed him."

"I work hard and I play hard."

MILAN SAYS "GLOVES!"

148

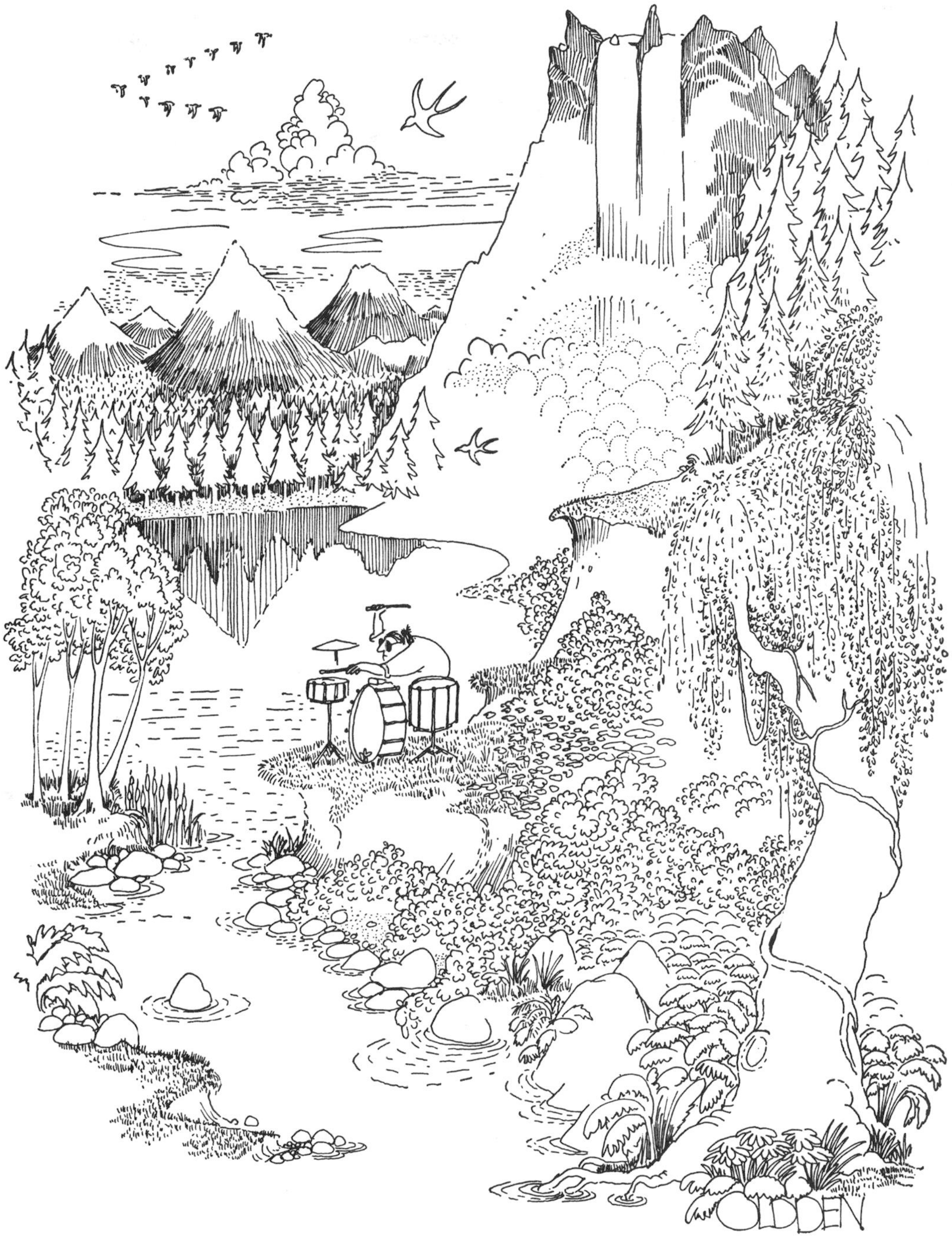
OLDDEN

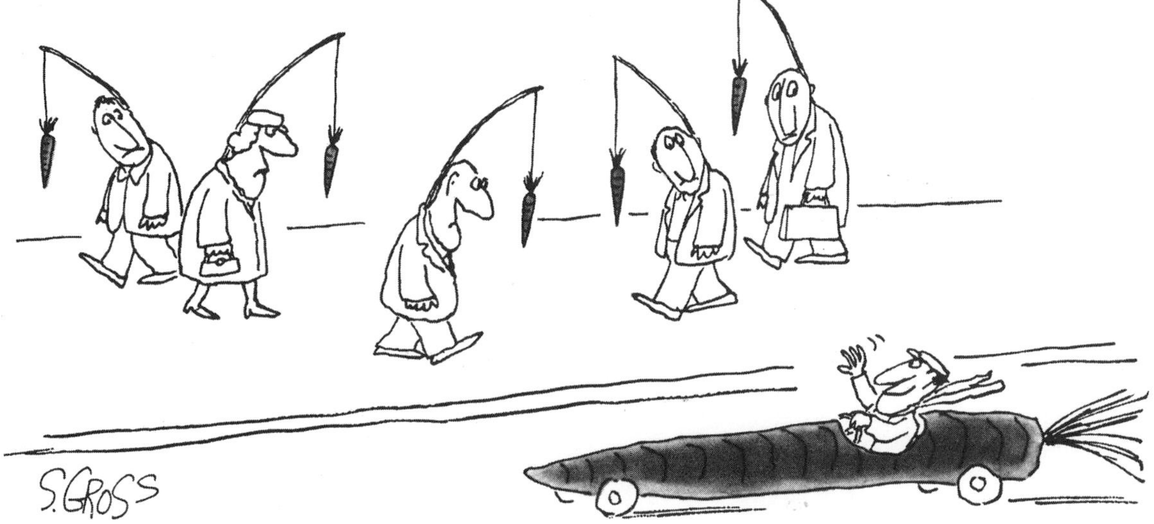
S. GROSS

"You smell like a chimney."

"Personally, I prefer a piano bar."

"Well, folks, here it is starting time!...
One moment while we take a look at that little old schedule."

"I'm sorry, dear, but you knew I was a bureaucrat when you married me."

*"Certainly. A party of four at seven–thirty in the name of Dr. Jennings.
May I ask whether that is an actual medical degree or a Ph.D.?"*

"Are you the one they call El Cóndor?"

"Boy, did $\underline{I}$ have an afternoon! The census man was here."

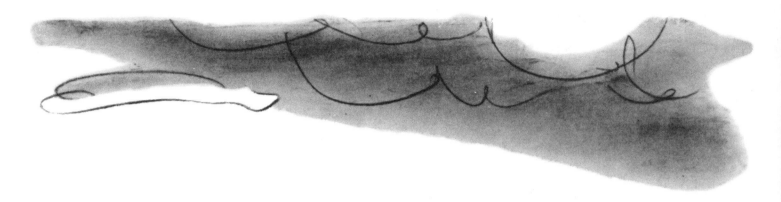

"Excuse me, sir. I am prepared to make you a rather attractive offer for your square."

"I can see this prepared as quenelles de maquereau with a nice rémoulade and some herbed zucchini spirals."

"Actually, I'm just coming down off a kind of surprising haircut, and I think I'll just hang around the house for a while."

"It isn't that I don't love you. It's just that I've evolved and you haven't."

"It was a very bleak period in my life, Louie. Martinis didn't help. Religion didn't help. Psychiatry didn't help. Transcendental meditation didn't help. Yoga didn't help. But Martinis helped a little."

"Would you like to hear some music while you hold?"

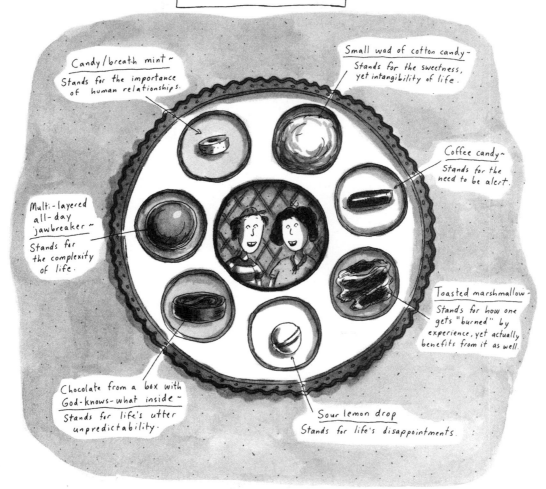

"Well, there she goes—the 5:08 to Los Angeles. Right on time!"

"Why am I talking this loud? Because I'm wrong."

"I'd just as soon it wasn't cut into those funny little pieces, if you don't mind."

"So far so good. Let's hope we win."

"I don't care if it's a boy or a girl, just as long as I'm healthy."

"Why do _you_ think you cross the road?"

"Don't worry. If it turns out tobacco is harmful, we can always quit."

"They're all sons of bitches."

"Joking or non-joking?"

"Oh, she's been acting that way all day.
Someone told her she looks like Katharine Hepburn."

"Mail is running three to one against our Christmas newsletter."

"Now, you wait right here while I go ask my wife for a divorce."

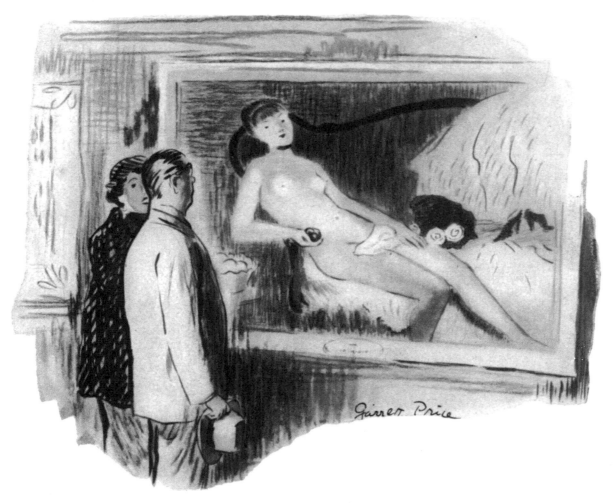

"Mama had a sofa just like that when we lived on South Elm Street."

FELICITÀ

"And I suppose cleaning up after yourself just once
would in some way stifle your precious creativity."

"I don't ask for much, but what I get should be of very good quality."

BAD MOM CARDS

COLLECT THE ENTIRE SET!

#4: ESTHER J.

Ran out of orange juice one morning and served kids orange soda instead.

#17: GLORIA B.

Promised to take daughter to the mall after school— and then _didn't_.

#20: JAYNE R.

Sent child to school with 99.1°F. temperature - and child _was_ sent home.

#23: LUCY L.

And then he...

Told friend "funny" story about kid and had a laugh at kid's expense.

#35: MARTINA F.

Didn't put up the St. Patrick's Day decorations one year.

#39: DAWN K.

When daughter left stuffed bear in Grand Union, waited until _next_ day to retrieve it.

#48: SUZIE M.

Let kid play two hours of Nintendo— _just to get him out of her hair._

#61: DEBORAH Z.

Has never even tried to make Play-Doh from scratch.

#89: BECKY O.

While on phone, told child to **SHUT THE HELL UP**, or she would brain her.

R. Chast

"Go down there and make them laugh."

KONG FOR A DAY

"Help! I'm being held prisioner!"

"Mind if I put on the game?"

*"Then it's moved and seconded that the
compulsory retirement age be advanced to ninety-five."*

"I agree he's a homicidal maniac, but I'm saluting the office, not the man."

"Of course I care about how you imagined I thought
you perceived I wanted you to feel."

"I'm back. The Brie's not ripe."

"I'm a social scientist, Michael. That means I can't explain electricity
or anything like that, but if you ever want to know about people I'm your man.

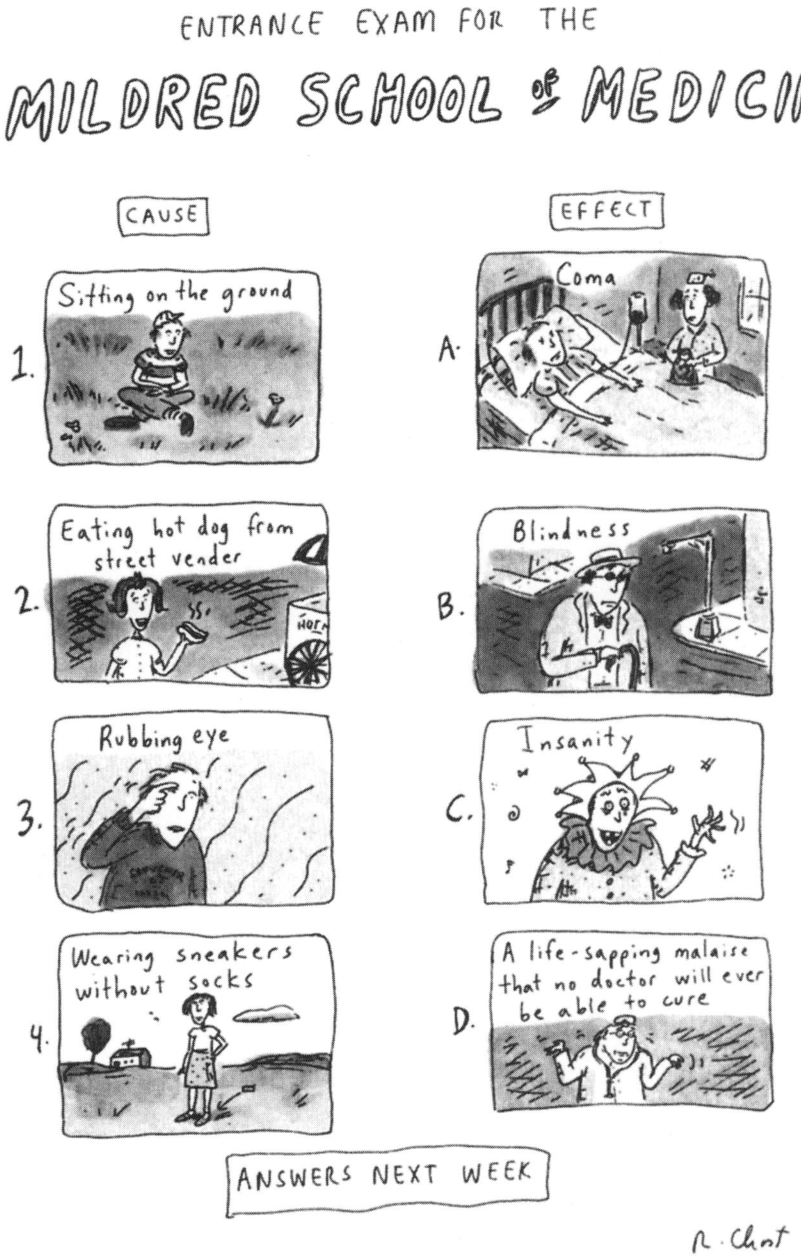
ENTRANCE EXAM FOR THE
MILDRED SCHOOL OF MEDICINE
CAUSE
EFFECT
1. Sitting on the ground
A. Coma
2. Eating hot dog from street vender
B. Blindness
3. Rubbing eye
C. Insanity
4. Wearing sneakers without socks
D. A life-sapping malaise that no doctor will ever be able to cure
ANSWERS NEXT WEEK
R. Chast

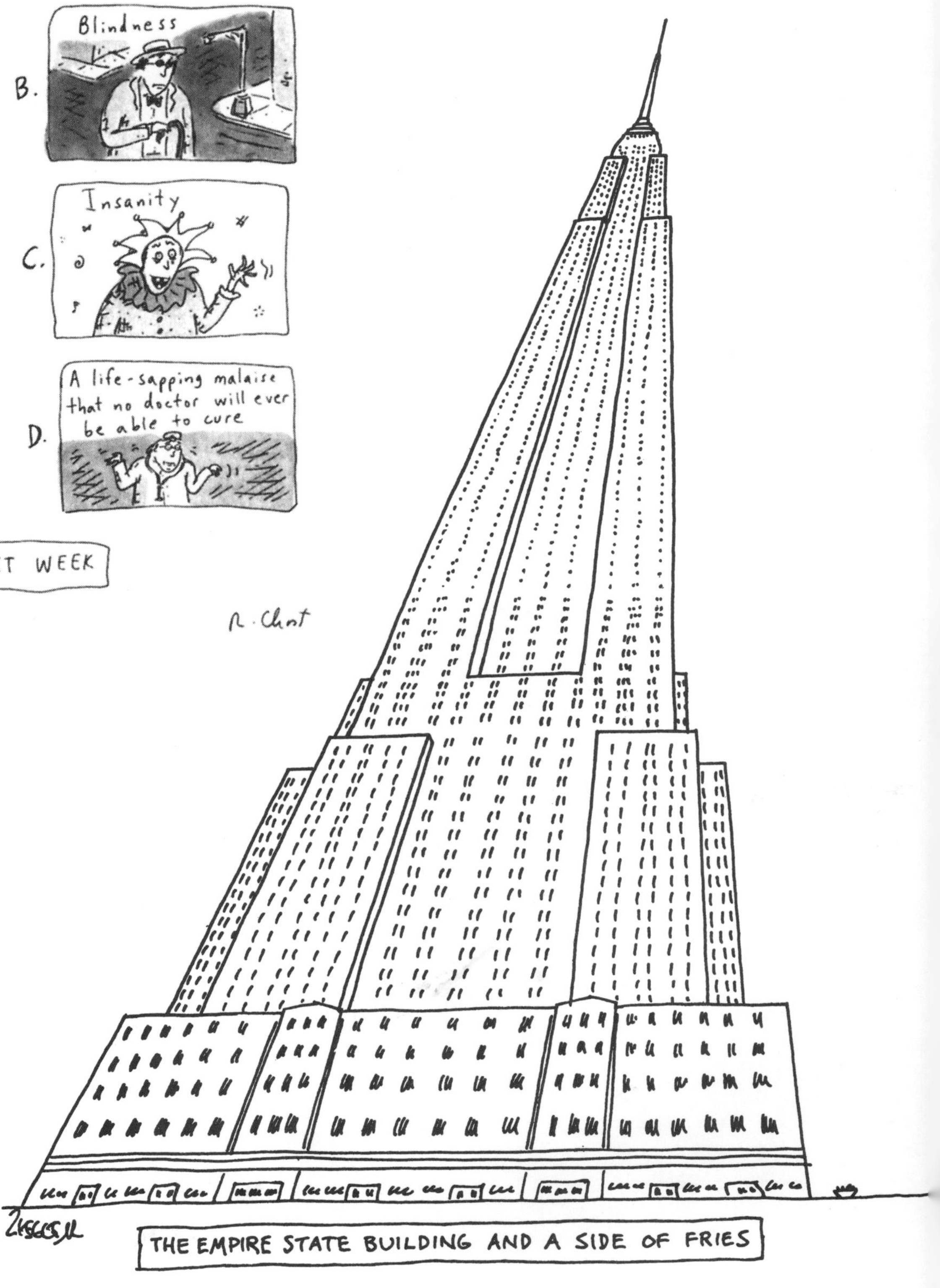

THE EMPIRE STATE BUILDING AND A SIDE OF FRIES

"What was that party against?"

"It's just the architect's model, but I'm very excited."

"Would you like to take your old face?"

"Excuse me, sir. Which way to Lexington Avenue?"

"I have a brief statement, a clarification, and two denials."

"Show me the way to the next karaoke bar."

"What's so great about due process?
Due process got me ten years."

"I have this recurring dream about
reclining on a bed of wild rice."

JANUARY 3RD AT ROCKEFELLER CENTER

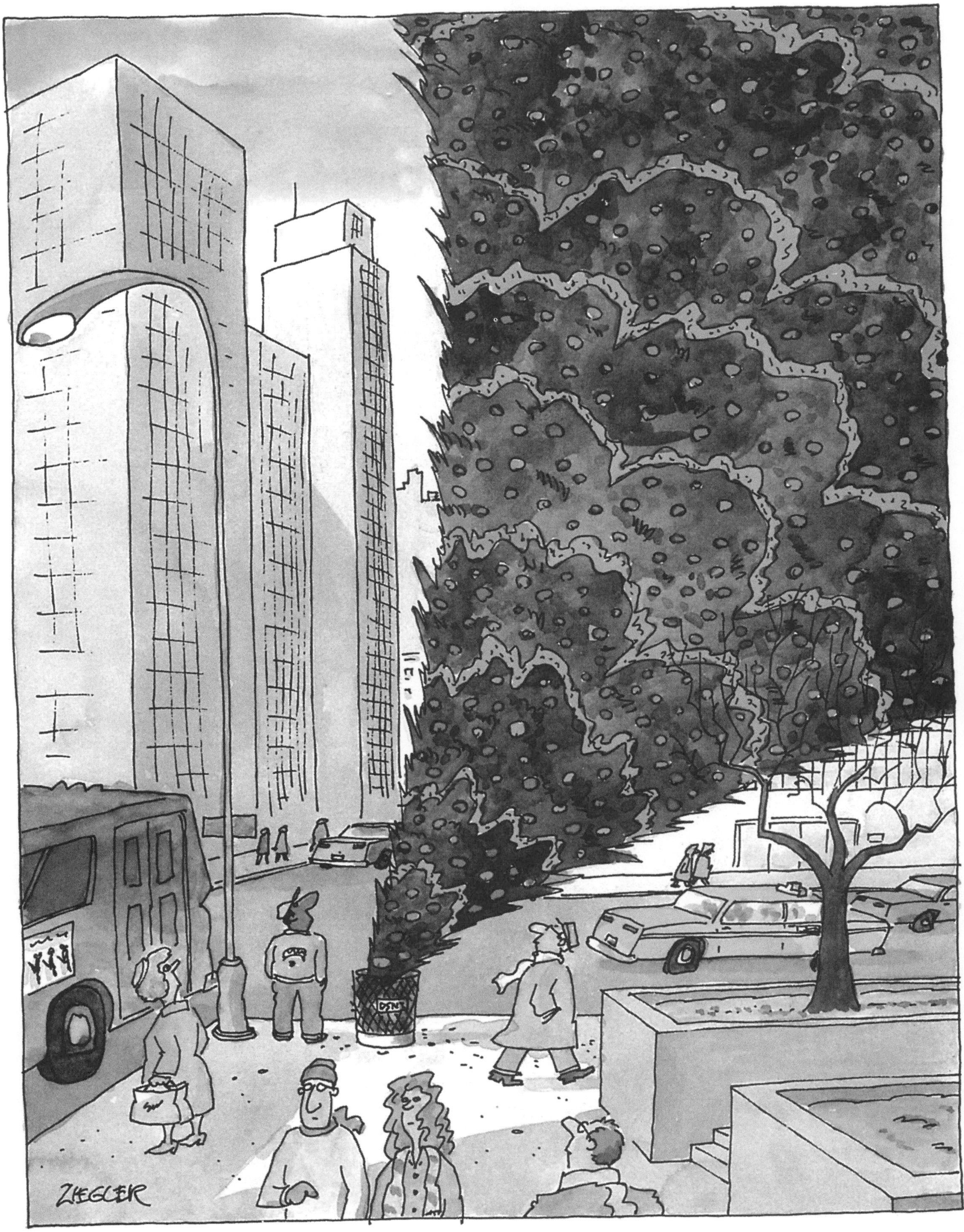
ZIEGLER

"If Heather has two mommies, and each of them has two brothers, and one of those brothers has another man for a 'roommate,' how many uncles does Heather have?"

"Never, ever, think outside the box."

"I never know when you're kidding."

"You blow a billion here, you blow
a billion there. It adds up."

"By George, you're right! I *thought* there was something familiar about it."

FOR THOSE WHO DON'T FEEL THAT DRIVING SCHOOL IS QUITE ENOUGH, THERE'S...

DRIVERS' UNIVERSITY!

IMAGINE: FOUR YEARS WITH NOTHING TO DO BUT <u>LEARNING TO DRIVE A CAR*</u>!

(* automatic)

THE CURRICULUM	
FIRST YEAR	• Getting to Know Cars: Where is the brake? Where is the gas pedal? Where is the ignition? How should I hold the wheel? etc.
SECOND YEAR	• All About Road Signs
THIRD YEAR	• Actual Driving: Small lanes, daytime, good weather • Beginning to Park
FOURTH YEAR	• Highway Driving. Night Driving, Driving in the Snow or Rain • Advanced Parking

REGISTER NOW, AND IN JUST FOUR YEARS

THIS COULD BE YOU!

I'm going to the store—does anybody need anything?

"Then what happened?"

"It's remarkable, Mr. Volmer. You have
the clothes of a man half your age!"

"I hope you don't mind. We're workaholics."

"Now look what you've done!"

"Alden, which of the five senses do you value most?"

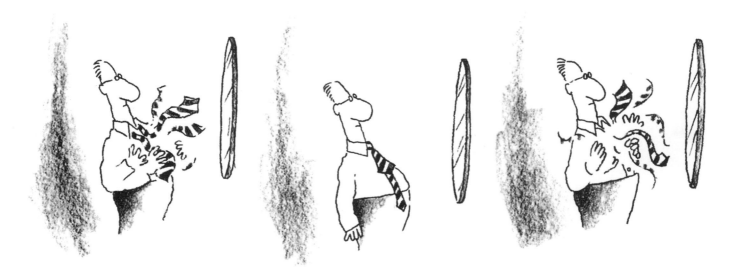

"There's no need for your kitty to be envious. After state and federal taxes and legal and administrative fees, Chessy's share of Aunt Martha's estate came to hardly anything."

"Each one is numbered, dated, and signed by the grower."

"If you're so enlightened, how come you can't lick that slice?"

"Wow! You need professional help."

"Combination No. 5—no MSG."

"Watch out, Fred! Here it comes again!"

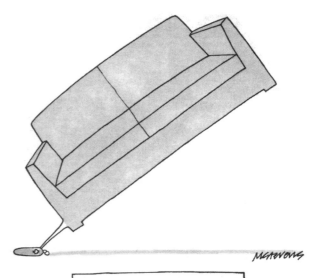

SWISS ARMY COUCH

"Now if we can all be silent for a few moments, we will hear the thunder of the waters."

"The ringing in your ears—I think I can help."

"It's always cozy in here.
We're insulated by layers of bureaucracy."

"Sorry, but I'm going to have to issue you a summons for reckless
grammar and driving without an apostrophe."

"It's not advertising anything, damn it!"

"I understand completely. I like good movies,
and you like bad movies."

"What's more important—that you don't catch cold
or that people don't laugh at you?"

IN A QUANDARY

The Voice of Reason:

It's not such a big thing, just put the galoshes on.

The Voice of Conscience:

Mom will be mad if you don't put them on.

The Voice of Practicality:

It's raining. Why don't you just wear 'em?

The Voice of Binky:

Toss them out of the window.

R. Chast

"Why, you're right. Tonight isn't reading night, tonight is sex night."

"I never thought I'd grow up
to be the matinée crowd."

"Nonsense, Mother. You'll probably outlive us all."

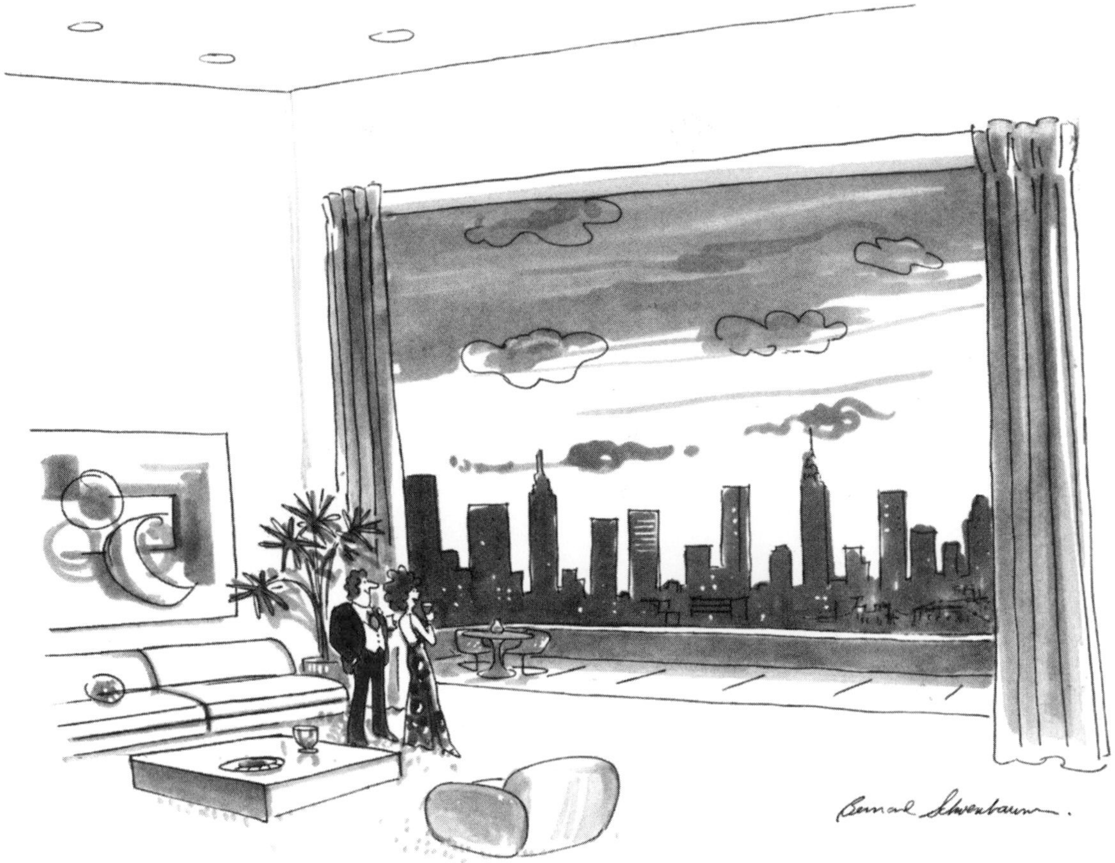

"I love it! It says city."

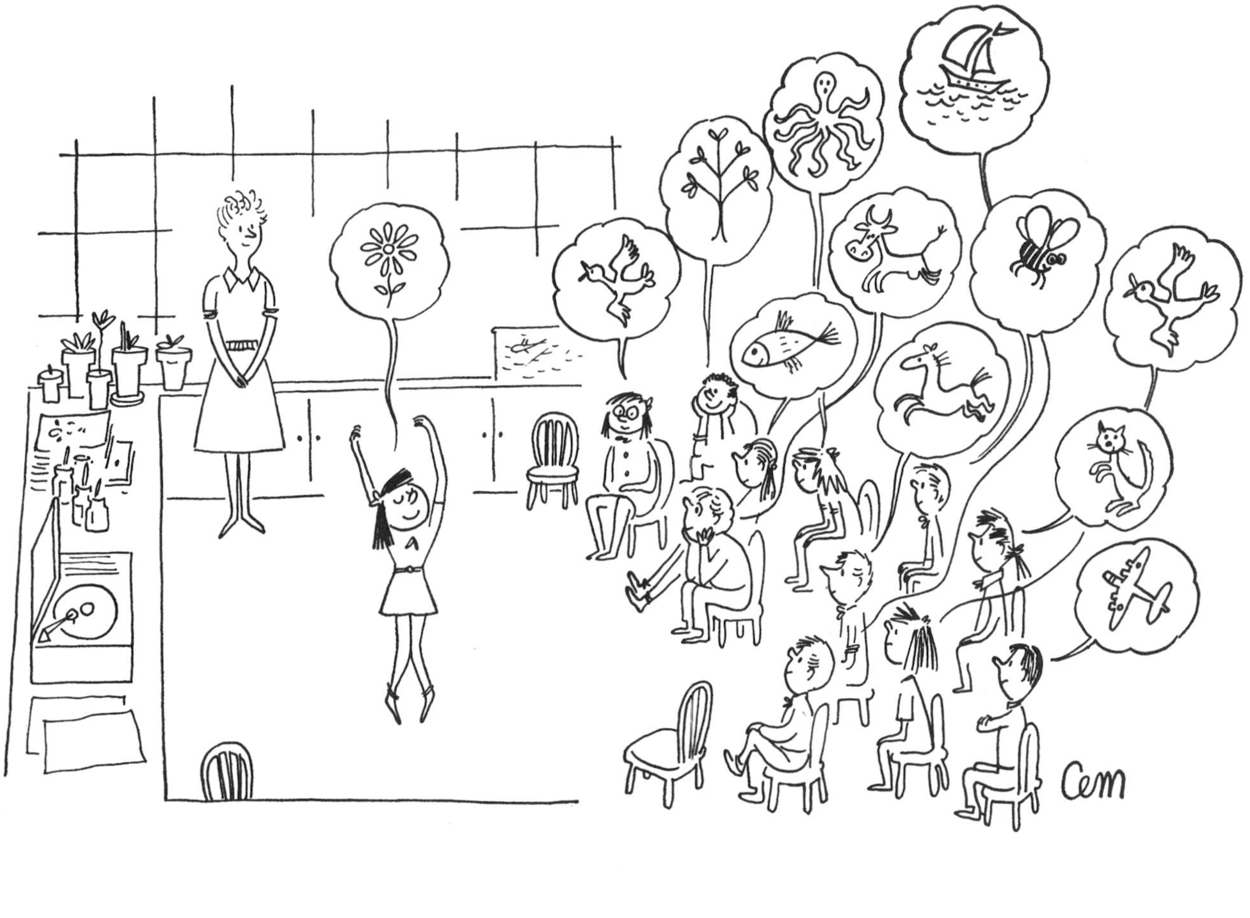

THE GRAND TETONS EN BUSTIER

"It's dull now, but at the end they smash their instruments and set fire to the chairs."

"As a matter of fact, you did catch us at a bad time."

"I'd like to see everything you have on girls."

"I've called the family together to announce that, because of inflation,
I'm going to have to let two of you go."

"The New Year is approaching, Miriam—traditionally a time of new beginnings.
I suggest we use the occasion to dedicate ourselves to restoring that atmosphere of trust and
mutual respect which characterized the early years of our marriage, and that in that spirit
we continue to work together toward what I sincerely hope will be an amicable divorce."

"'Honesty is the best policy.' O.K.!
Now, what's the second-best policy?"

"Captain, this Brie is totally out of control!"

"Well, if I called the wrong number, why did you answer the phone?"

BEES

WORKER

QUEEN

DRONE

CONSULTANT

"This 'road not taken' where we're going for dinner, was she also a road not travelled?"

"They have this arrangement. He earns the money and she takes care of the house."

"You and your 'just one more tap'!"

"It's a bedtime story. It doesn't <u>need</u> corroboration."

"I hope you don't mind. He doesn't know he's a dog."

"George Stoner is here from Terre Haute. He and Henry are talking over old times."

*"I think the vomitorium would look terrific in
Pompeiian red, don't you?"*

"It's very simple. If I was a cat, you would love me."

"Why don't you slip into your shooting jacket with the bellows pockets and the double shoulder patches and nip down to the corner for a quart of milk?"

"We're through, do you hear? Through! Washed up! Kaput!"

"Don't say a word! Your eyes, your hair, your T-shirt, your luggage—they say it all."

"What burns me up is that the answer is right here somewhere, staring us in the face."

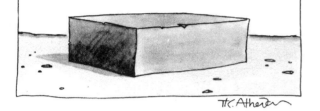

FOUR HUNDRED SELECTIONS OF THE WORLD'S FINEST ORCHESTRAL MUSIC, OVER ONE THOUSAND FULL-COLOR REPRODUCTIONS OF MANKIND'S GREATEST PAINTINGS AND SCULPTURE, AND TWO HUNDRED AND THIRTY-ONE TIMELESS CLASSICS OF WESTERN LITERATURE COMPACTED INTO A TWO-BY-THREE-BY-SIX-INCH BRICK.

"Remember, Kimberly, I'm more than your agent. I'm your mother."

"No, I don't want to play chess. I just want you to reheat the lasagna."

"You call that hung by the chimney with care?"

"I'll have an ounce of prevention."

"I'm not asking you to change your spots.
I'm just asking you to take out the garbage."

"I don't feel the pea anymore, but that condom wrapper is killing me."

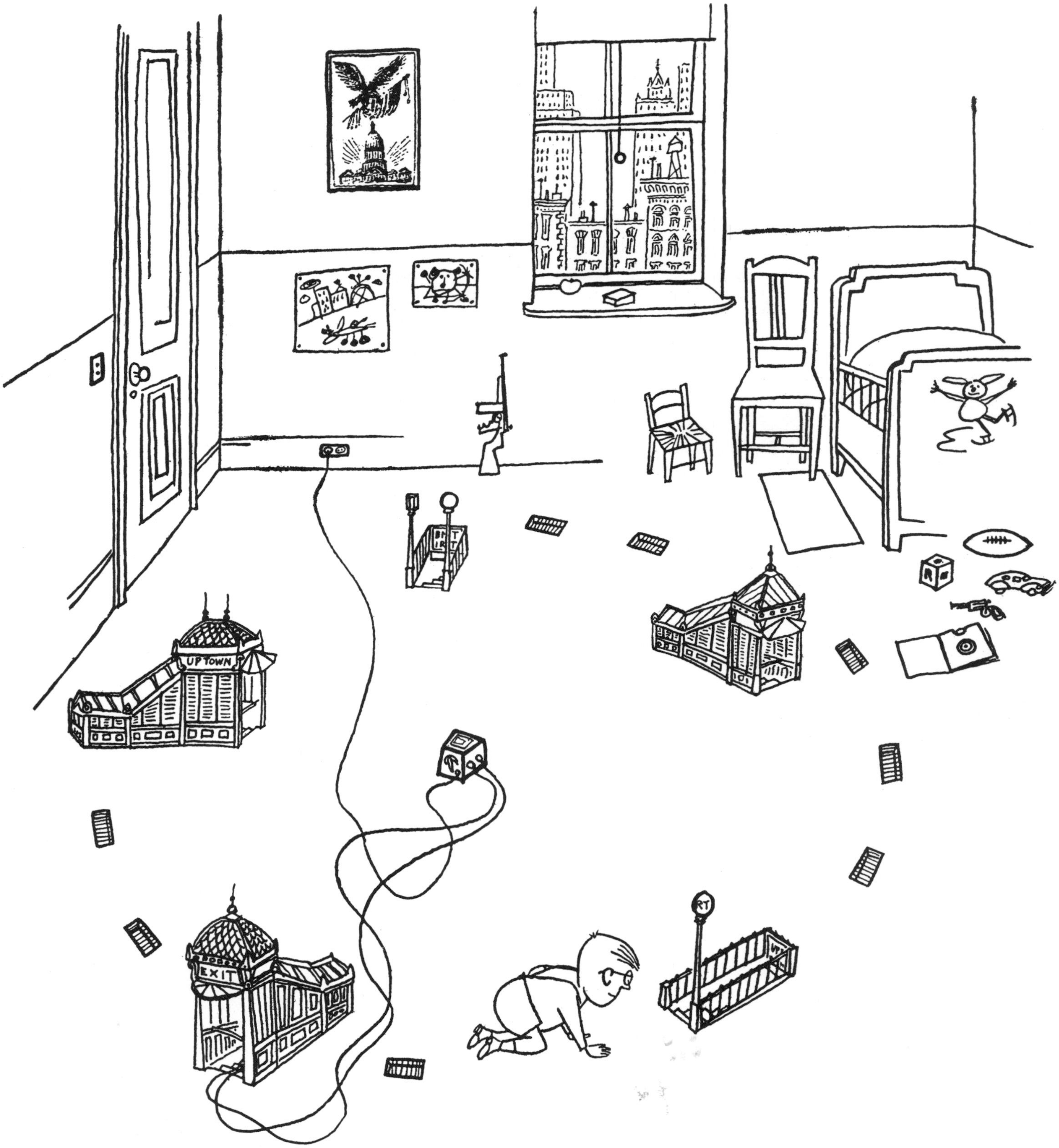
UP TOWN
EXIT
STEINBERG

HOW THE STEALTH BOMBER EVADES RADAR

"Just a trim. Keep it about 486–480 B.C."

"I love the convenience, but the roaming charges are killing me."

"Hey, everybody,
we're invited to a cookout!"

"I can't decide whether to specialize
in criminal law or legal punditry."

"We love the view. It helps to remind us that
we're part of a larger community."

"It's publish or perish, and he hasn't published."

"No, no, Senator, no thanks are necessary at this time."

"It appears to be Siva, manifesting himself as Lord of Destruction,
but why he's in Hartsdale on a Thursday night is beyond me."

"I tell you there isn't going to be any insurrection."

"I will not talk to myself, I will not talk to myself."

"Actually, I preferred 'Heaven,' too,
but then the marketing guys got hold of it."

"For God's sake, Edwards. Put the laser pointer away."

"Gentlemen, being a superpower is no longer enough.
We must become a super–duper power."

"*Most successful suit sale we ever had, I should say.*"

"Haven't you ever seen California wine being made before?"

"Relax, honey—change is good."

"Why can't they save all the commercials to the end,
and then we could be honor-bound to look at them?"

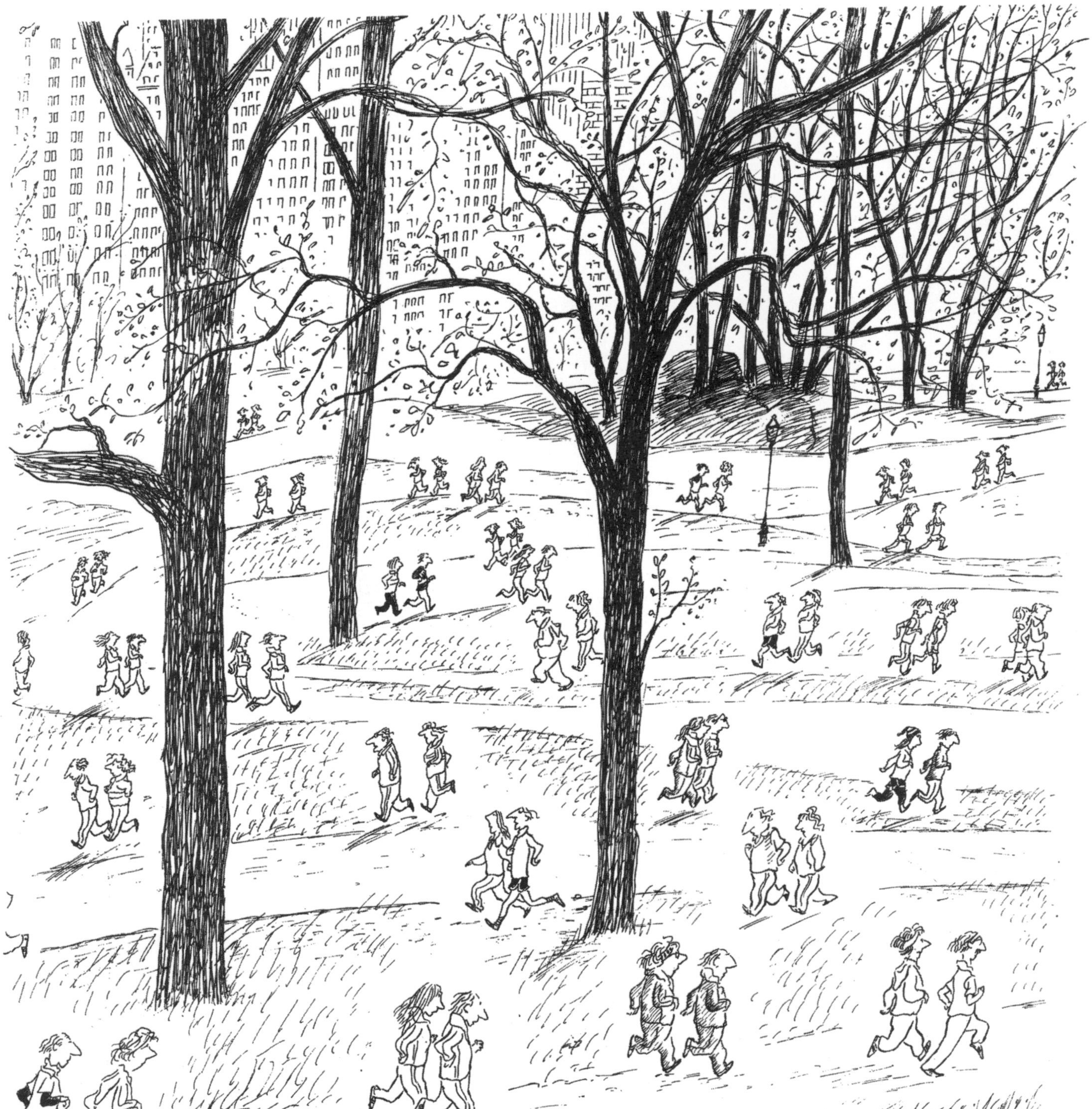
sempé

"Anything wrong?"

"Oh, the usual. Lunch at Le Cirque and then the abyss."

"Don't worry about me. I'm a survivor."

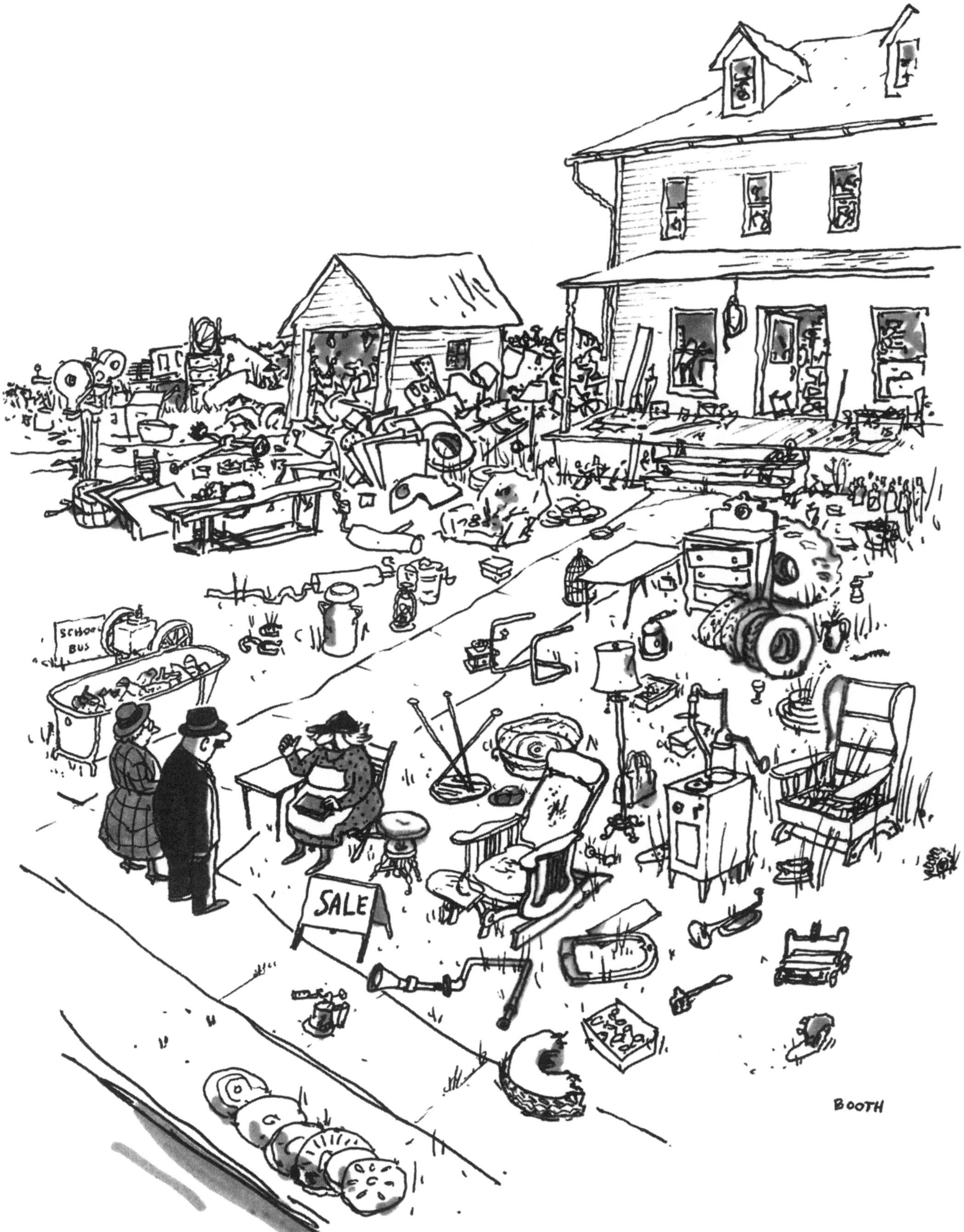
SCHOOL BUS
SALE
BOOTH

"There's more inside."

Shanahan

"Finally, we realized where all
that anger was coming from."

"An excellent defense.
Let's give her the doctorate."

"I believe I'll skip the appetizer. I ate the flowers."

"And, in this corner, weighing five pounds more than she'd like . . ."

"No, lad, we aren't movers. We're just Shakers."

NICE WORK, CHARLEY

"I wonder if the 'Harvard Classics' are still up there. Yep, there they are."

"We've thought and thought, but we're at a loss about what to call ourselves. Any ideas?"

"I dreamed last night that we two-hundred-dollared Mr. Ferguson to death."

"Gimme a break. Being driven out of Ireland was the best thing that ever happened to you."

MODERN MEDICINE

"Well, Bob, it looks like a paper cut, but just to be sure let's do lots of tests."

"I hear we've just been granted most-favored-nation status."

"It's a love story. Nobody's ahead."

"Our _real_ first line of defense, wouldn't you agree,
is our capacity to reason."

"All right, have it your way—you heard a seal bark."

*"Hello? Beasts of the Field? This is Lou, over in Birds of the Air.
Anything funny going on over at your end?"*

"It's so much easier now that the children are our age."

"Gee, you're not at all like your obituaries."

"It's only the wind."

225

"We found her wandering at the edge of the forest.
She was raised by scientists."

"Bertha, will you do me a favor and stop reading those damn 'How to Save Your Marriage' articles?"

"Love to stay, but we have a sitter."

"Teri tells me you're ostensibly straight."

"Well, it was sort of like a cook-out."

"So what'll it be tonight—pig in or pig out?"

"O.K., who has to go potty before we disappear into the Federal Witness Protection Program?"

"My son the lawyer is suing my son the doctor for malpractice."

"This is the time of year when you begin to appreciate the 'Times's' fuller coverage."

"Now, which one of the Thousand Islands is this?"

THE SEVEN DWARFS AFTER THERAPY

"Oh dear, the bell! We have to go back."

"Waiter, I'd like to order, unless I've eaten,
in which case bring me the check."

"Washington, New York; New York, Boston;
Boston, Washington. How was _your_ day?"

"What a delightful surprise. I always thought it just trickled down to the poor."

"I never told her about the Depression. She would have worried."

"We used to entertain a great deal."

"I thought it was me, but maybe the school's no damn good."

"Winning is crucial to my retirement plans."

"The men are excited about getting to shoot a lawyer."

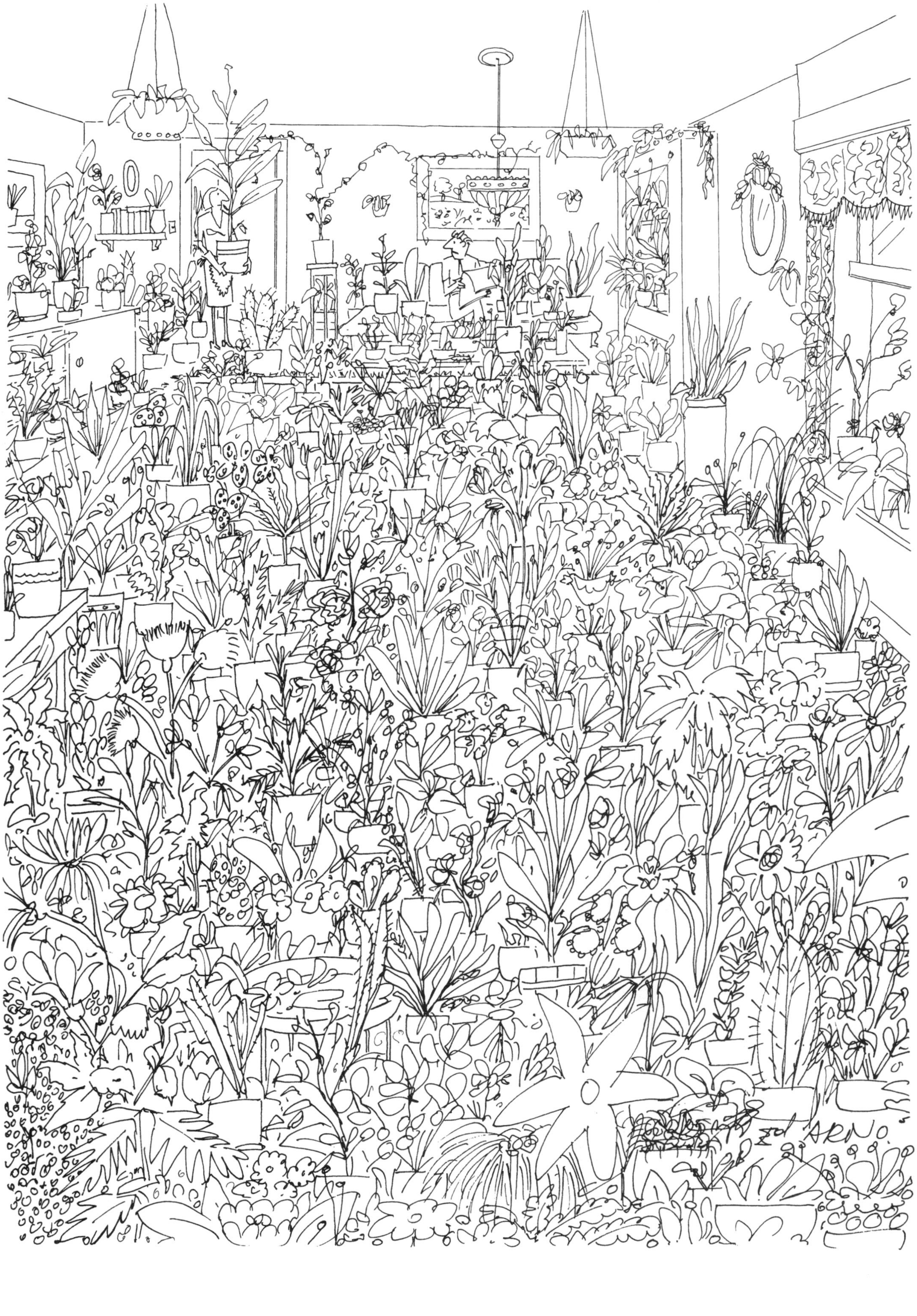
ARNO

"No, no, no—stay as late as you want. In fact, divorce me."

TREASURE MAP

"Remember to mention how we miss the change of seasons in L. A.
It means so much to people who are still back here in New York."

"This is my favorite part of our summer vacation—when you lean into the wind."

"I don't think you can distance yourself from the White House on this one. After all, you are the President."

"The economy's never been better. Here's another potato!"

"If I take back what I said about your pants, will you let me go?"

"This is Mrs. McBride from marketing."

"Sorry, no water. We're just a support group."

A Pause in the Conversation

"Popcorn's done, honey."

"Give me more angels and make them gladder to see me."

STATESMAN
PATRIOT
APPREHENDED

"We'll have to go around the Horn. They won't take a check."

"I've got the bowl, the bone, the big yard. I know I _should_ be happy."

"Women kiss women good night.
Men kiss women good night.
But men do not kiss men good night—
especially in Armonk."

"No, Thursday's out. How about never—is never good for you?"

"I _love_ the Caribbean in February!"

"I must confess I've noticed your stopping by for a drink,
but I never dreamed you'd noticed me."

W. Steig

Dear Jacqueline, As you probably already know, I love you

"Oh, yes, we know them. We hate them."

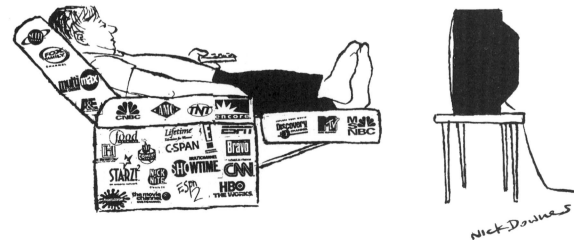

Nick Downes

"You were sensational."

"My wife! My best friend! My favorite TV program!"

"I've got an idea for a story: Gus and Ethel live on Long Island, on the North Shore.
He works sixteen hours a day writing fiction. Ethel never goes out, never does anything except fix
Gus sandwiches and in the end she becomes a nympho-lesbo-killer-whore. Here's your sandwich."

"Say, pal, how the hell do we get off this scenic route?"

RECIPES
from the
AMERICAN CHEESE COUNCIL

Cheese Omelette

2 eggs
5 lb. Swiss cheese
1 tbsp. butter

Melt butter in pan. Add eggs and cheese. Cook until done. Serves 2.

Cheese Salad

1 tomato
1 mushroom
1 leaf of lettuce
2 lb. cheddar
1 lb. Muenster

1 lb. feta cheese
1 lb. blue cheese
1 lb. Parmesan
½ lb. Camembert
½ lb. Gruyère

Make everything bite-sized, then place in bowl. Serves 6 cheese-loving people.

Cheese Patties

6 lb. soft cheese

Form cheese into patties. Serve on a bun. Makes enough for 12 patties.

Cheese Pick-Me-Up

½ cup water
1 lb. Brie

Put everything in blender at a high speed. Serve immediately. Just enough for one.

R.Chast

"'To Mario—Good food, good fun.
Thanks. Leonardo da Vinci.'"

"Damn it, I _am_ looking pleasant!"

"Well, there goes Junior."

"If you're so good, why can't you ever
strike twice in the same place?"

"You may well be from Mars, but the children
and I are still from Westchester."

CHILDREN'S PERSONALS

NEW IN NBRHD -
Just moved in. Girl, 9, wishes to meet other girls, 8-10. Likes Barbie, Ken, Skipper. Box 101.

BOY W/ICKY PARENTS - I need a rebellious peer group, ages 10-12. Serious replies only. Box 215.

GIRL, 4, LOOKING FOR IMGNRY FRIEND - Humans need not apply. Photo a must. Box 643.

R. Chast

"You'll have to excuse my wife. She's a bit of a control freak."

"That will be Williams with your Twinkie."

"*Give us this day no sonic boom.*"

CHICKEN À LA KING

"Your daughter is a pain in the ass."

"Thank goodness you're here. His dish is empty."

"I *do* think your problems are serious, Richard.
They're just not very interesting."

"How very exciting! I have never before met a
Second Amendment lawyer."

PYRAMID CLUB

CHARLIE CHAPLIN

LAUREL   HARDY

LARRY   MOE   CURLY

GROUCHO   CHICO   HARPO   ZEPPO

THE HOUSE OF REPRESENTATIVES

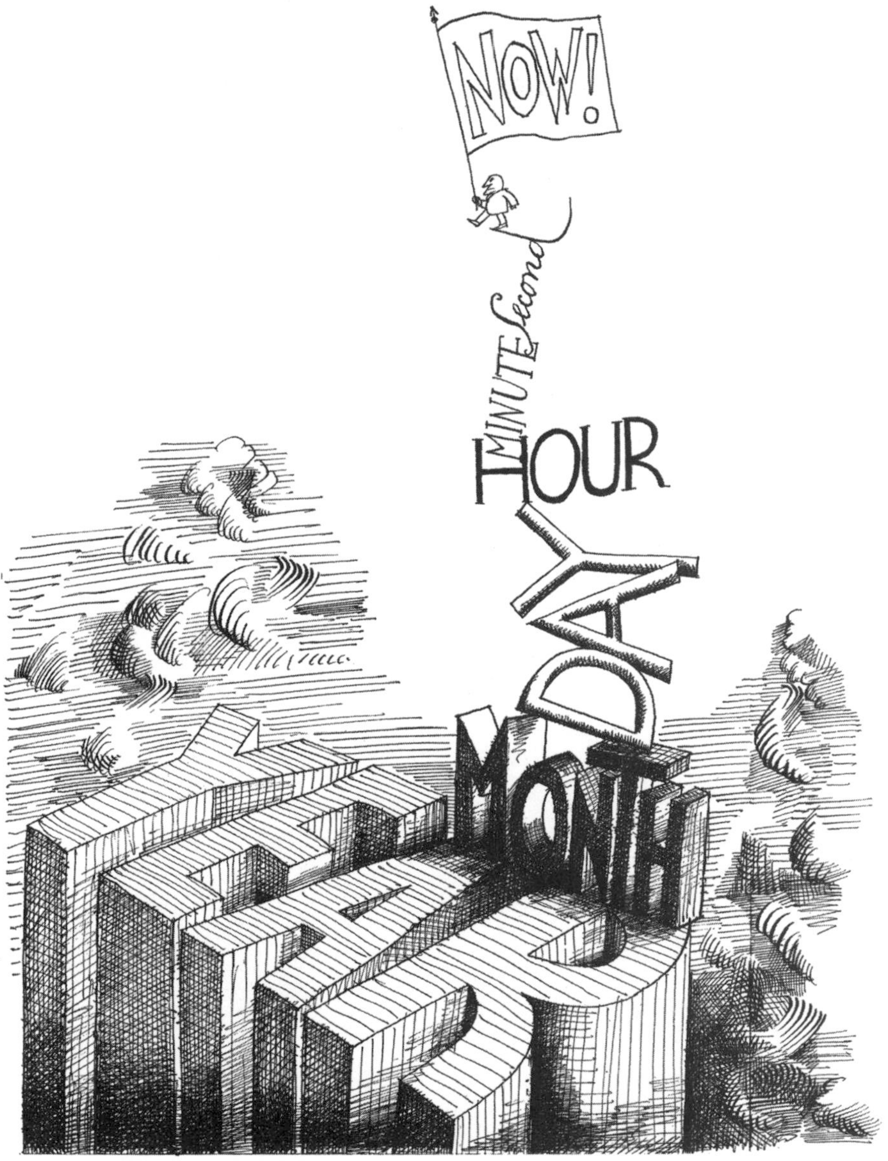
NOW!
Second
MINUTE
HOUR
DAY
MONTH
YEAR

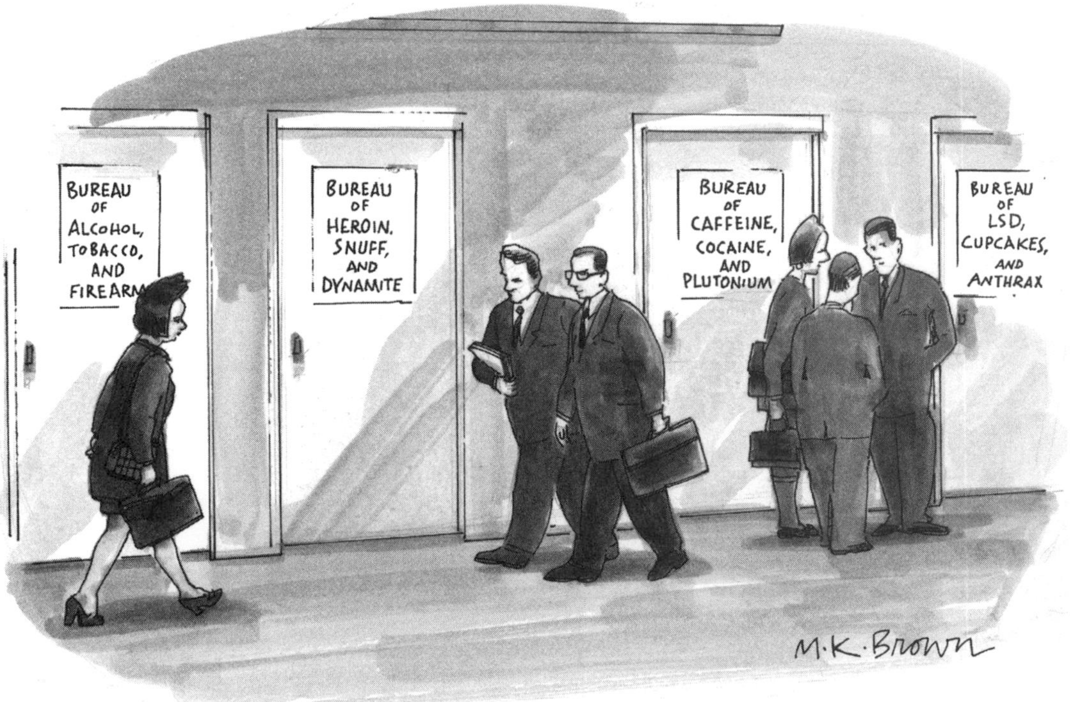
BUREAU OF ALCOHOL, TOBACCO, AND FIREARM
BUREAU OF HEROIN, SNUFF, AND DYNAMITE
BUREAU OF CAFFEINE, COCAINE, AND PLUTONIUM
BUREAU OF LSD, CUPCAKES, AND ANTHRAX
M.K. Brown

"Look at it this way, Conroy—the longer they stay out, the longer you're a free man."

"Perfect."

"Hi, I'm the tooth fairy.
Want to buy back some of your teeth?"

"Could you walk a little faster, buddy? This is New York."

"We could never have done it without him."

"No, I don't. And I'll tell you why."

"He's my best friend and he works hard all day.
Couldn't you at least wag your tail?"

"I'm undecided, but that doesn't mean
I'm apathetic or uninformed."

"Frieze!"

"Now you and I are going to share a little secret."

"For God's sake, think! Why is he being so nice to you?"

"Either cheer up or take off the hat."

"Which one is the love potion?"

"I just want to say that I'm perfectly willing to serve as treasurer, provided every penny doesn't have to come out exactly even."

"Every man for himself!"

263

"Maynard, I do think that just this once you should come out and see the moon!"

"Well, I do have this recurring dream
that one day I might see some results."

"I'm down to two hundred and sixty-three packs a day."

"It's not you, Rob. It's just that things are moving a little too fast."

"It is wonderful, comma, sir, comma, how rare a quality good humor is in life, full stop. We meet with very few good-humored men, full stop."

"Of course you're going to be depressed if you keep comparing yourself with successful people."

"All we can do now is sit tight and pray."

"On the other hand, the Maitlands went by tramp steamer and loved every minute of it."

"Hi. I'm, I'm, I'm... You'll have to forgive me,
I'm terrible with names."

"I take it, General Sedgewick, you're about to propose a surgical strike."

CAB FROM HELL

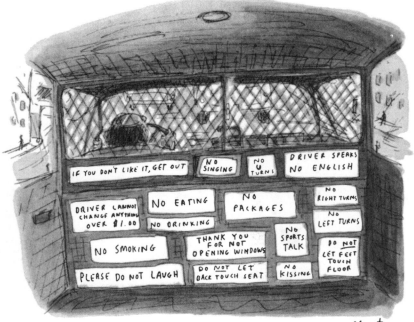

R. Chast

"His will reads as follows: 'Being of sound mind and disposition, I blew it all.'"

"The father belonged to some people who were driving through in a Packard."

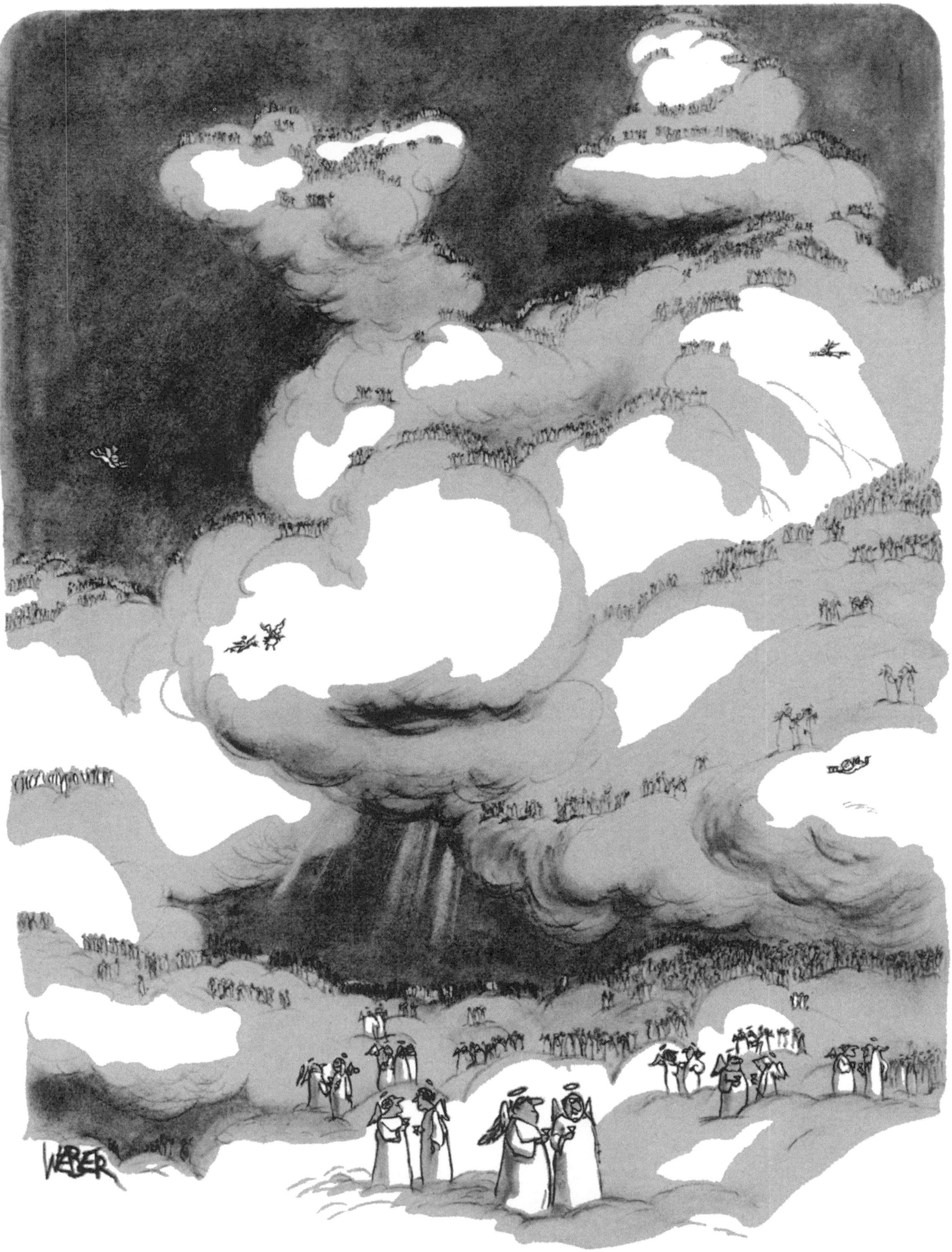
WEBER

"Superb Martinis!"

"The wattle fairy came again last night."

"What gear are we in, biscuit?"

"What's amazing to me is that this late in the game we _still_ have to settle our differences with rocks."

"I've had a long talk with Jonah,
and I think he's willing to work with us."

"It's the children, darling—back from camp."

"Touché!"

"On the Internet, nobody knows you're a dog."

"I'm so hungry I could eat half a sandwich."

"And this one is my grandma and her current lover."

"If I may, Mr. Perlmutter, I'd like to answer your question _with_ a question."

"Oh, for goodness' sake! Smoke!"

"You never remember __my__ birthday!"

THE DIALOGUES OF PLATO

FROM

Phrieda:	Plato, what do you want for lunch?
Plato:	Anything. Whatever.
Phrieda:	How's tuna?
Plato:	Not tuna.
Phrieda:	I could make you some scrambled eggs.
Plato:	Grilled cheese.
Phrieda:	We don't have any cheese.
Plato:	I want *grilled cheese*!
Phrieda:	I'll go to the store later and buy some cheese, but right now we don't have any cheese, so tell me: what do you want for lunch?
Plato:	I don't want anything.
Phrieda:	You have to have something.
Plato:	You can't force me.

STOPPOS & SHOPPOS

r. aw

"Here's the guest room. Just make yourselves at home."

"Hey, what about dames?"

"Dad, when did you realize you weren't, you know, exactly studly anymore?"

"Oh, I've had a few failures, followed by a string of successful marriages."

"I've been thinking—it might be good for Andrew
if he could see you cry once in a while."

"I thought I loved it, but Gordon said
we were just manipulated."

REQUIEM FOR A LIGHTWEIGHT

"*Location, location, location.*"

"Look, if you can't stand the Byzantine intrigue, perhaps you should get out of the cabal."

"It's a mixed blessing."

"I'm sorry, we've had to drop the traditional last cigarette,
on account of complaints from the firing squad about secondhand smoke."

"Hey, Mac. If you want sunshine, why don't you go sit in the park?"

"Whistle, you dumb bastard!"

"And, while there's no reason yet to panic,
I think it only prudent that we make preparations to panic."

"That's the trouble with pets. They're so destructive."

285

"Why, no. I've never thought of putting funny little captions on the bottom."

"Do you want to stay for the credits?"

INDEX

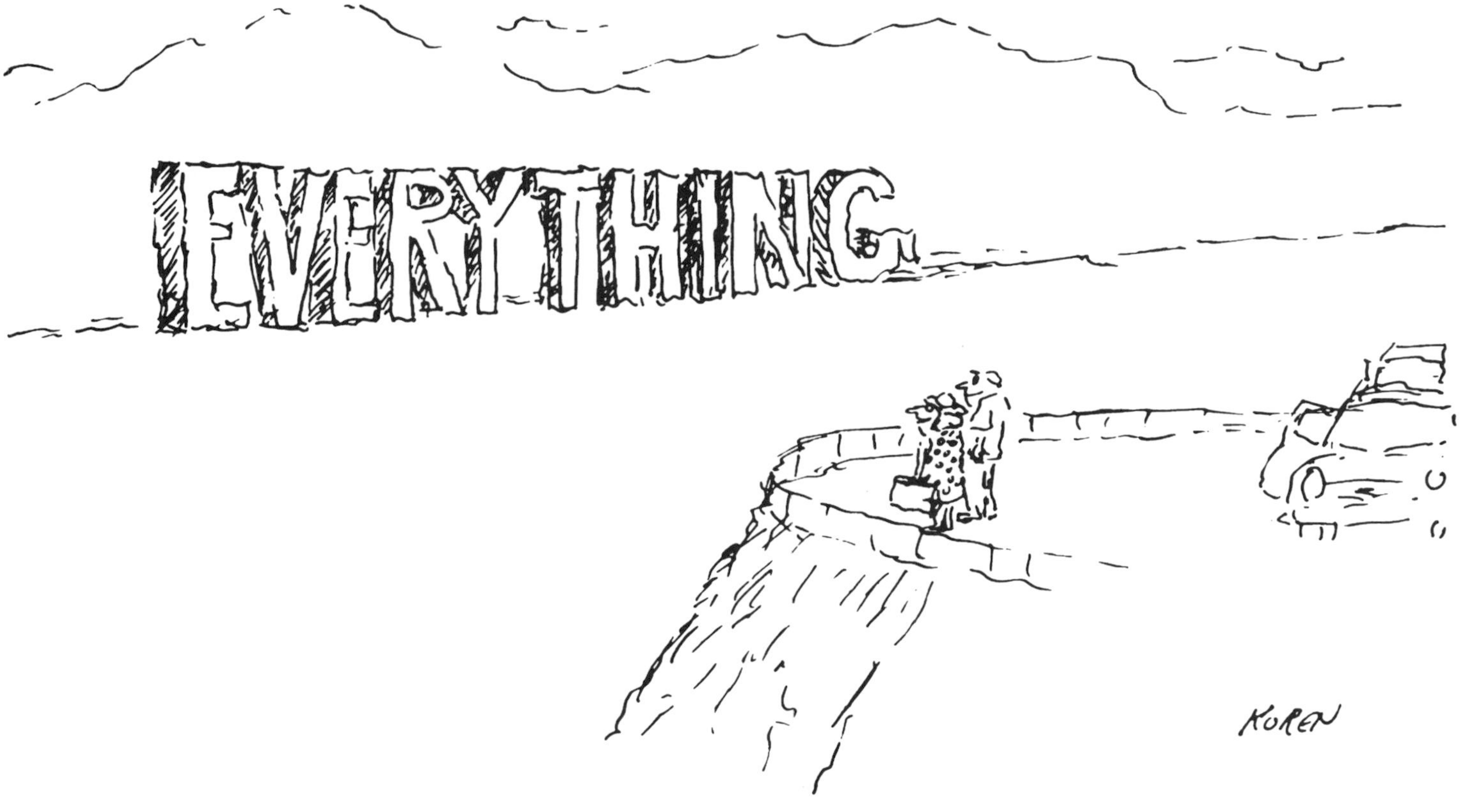
EVERYTHING
KOREN

"Now we've seen it."